PROFILES
of SUCCESS

PROFILES
of SUCCESS

Bridge-Logos *Publishers*

North Brunswick, New Jersey 08902 USA

Cover photograph of Larry Burkett is by kind permission of Travis Massey, Magic Craft Studios

Profiles of Success

Edited by Ronnie Belanger & Brian Mast
Copyright © 1999
by Bridge-Logos Publishers
Library of Congress Catalog Number: 99-64057
ISBN: 0-88270-775-2

Published by:
Bridge-Logos *Publishers*
North Brunswick Corporate Center
1300 Airport Road, Suite E
North Brunswick, NJ 08902

CONTENTS

CHARACTER & INTEGRITY

INVESTING BIBLICAL PRINCIPLES

Leadership & Management

Marriage & Family

Motivating Change

Personal Growth

PREFACE

Would you like to know some inside tips for being successful? Have you any dreams of being "your own boss," making it to the top? Are you interested in seeing the world marketplace positively impacted by the standards of Christ? Is there someone in the forefront of the Christian marketplace that you've just got to know more about?

As you read through this book you will be immersed in a world so full of interest, life's joys, sorrows and triumphs that, if you're anything like me, you won't be able to put it down!

I can truly say, "I've read every article in every edition of *The Christian Businessman* magazine, and oh, by the way I'm a girl!" "Not such a big deal," you might reply, but the depth and scope of the literature presented to the avid reader is not to be overlooked. Mr. Guy Carlson and his editor Brian Mast have been releasing, month after month, magazines with vision and scope. Magazines that catch the essence of Christianity in the workplace and elevate it to an attainable walk with the Lord on our road to success and fulfillment. When the publisher, here at Bridge-Logos, Guy Morrell, met with these gentlemen, the idea for this project was formed. As the reading research began, I asked myself, "What do you expect from someone you'd call a Christian? How can I help others recognize the qualities needed for their success? What would I like to share with other Christians I now know in the workplace?" From those perspectives this book began to take its shape.

Working in the Christian marketplace, might seem easier to some, a getaway from the hectic world of business in the "real world," but after a few years in the Christian business market's trenches, it can be seen that if you are to verbally admit you are a Christian, you must, I feel, be saying something far beyond the common realm of everyday workplace experiences.

There are many workers in the Christian marketplace who are truly servicing other Christians, but the standards of Christ, integrity, forthrightness, trustworthiness and honor are somewhat lacking or only observed while there is an audience available for the noticing.

Learning and stretching ourselves to succeed beyond the commonplace is what this compilation of fine articles and feature stories is all about.

We must examine each gem and pearl given within these covers for they are offered by the "best of the best." Let's just mention and acknowledge, for a moment, a few of the authors that really stand-out in this volume. Edwin Louis Cole for his continued direction and example as a "Major Among Men"; Larry Burkett for his firm foundational guidance, "Faithful on All Accounts," and his dedication to the application of biblical principles in the marketplace; Michael Pink's insightful view as he helps in our "Selling Among Wolves"; John Maxwell on Leadership and Wes Cantrell's "Promoting the Standard" will set your eyes above the horizon and on attainable heights. "Success is More than a Name" is a powerful article on Zig Ziglar, another man who's lived what he's preached and has his achievements to prove it. The section on Personal Growth including such pearls as, "The Sky's Not the Limit," from John Mason, Truett Cathy, Chic-fil-A's founder, speaks in the article, "Truett's Way," on his vision even for the growth of his employees. This section on our growth is a clincher for us all, for without it none of us go forward in our walk with the Lord, and we cannot go forward before all nations as witnesses of His glory.

Be sure to read about Pat Robertson, his beginnings and his triumphs! Dick DeVos, as President of Amway takes up his father's business success and carries it forward. See for yourself how former US Senator Bill Armstrong kept and maintained his image and witness for Christ in the political arena. We are told to "hold high the standard" for all to see our light shining upon a hill. It is written that people perish without a vision and a plan. Therefore, we must not only know the Scriptures, but we must live them. It's hard to ignore the world's chiding on the "marketing of Jesus Christ," but if we as a Christian Industry were ever to practice not just preach or occasionally demonstrate these qualities, the impact on our relationship with our Lord, our families, our communities, and our world would be earth-shattering!

Please do not think this volume has been put together without a hefty section devoted to our families and marriages. Guy Carlson has published a string of pearls on this very important fiber in our lives. It has grieved me to know that the divorce rate among Christians is as high as it is elsewhere, and for that purpose I've tried to include every helpful hint I could find in all of these magazines that could bless a couple and help them keep their marriage and family intact and growing healthily. Workers in this Christian community get their priorities messed up on a regular basis, yes we love to have our Christian ministries, but when that ministry or job is costing our family, either from our over-commitment, or our inability to change our direction and priorities we are running a muck with one of the great gifts from God—our spouse and our children.

Here then, for your very enjoyment, perusal, and edification are the greatest, most successful "Christian Entrepreneurs!" says A. L. Andrews. Each section is chocked full of step-by-step advice, real life trails and triumphs, exceptional tips for your personal life's applications, helpful hints to improving your walk with the Lord, your service to Him, your family and your ministry. For as Phil Downer writes we can make a difference, each one of us can touch one life at a time.

This is more than just a re-release of articles, each has been chosen and placed in one of the six sections as demonstrations and examples of the qualities needed for our success. A Christian in the marketplace has a life that is filled with challenges and demands that should exceed the commonplace for as Christians we must align ourselves with the precepts of God, hold ourselves to His standard, compromise less, wheel and deal honestly, keep relationships with our families alive and flourishing, treat our fellow workers and assistants in respectful regard, and then with all this our drive to succeed must not be diminished.

Remembering that God is still on the throne, He knows the beginning from the end is a comfort, and in this workplace that is our anchor whatever the trial, but we have a larger obligation here than most. We must be able to let the world see Him in all that we do.

No small task. No way to do this job halfway. Do you know a successful Christian? Now I do, I've read about them, their ministries, and their lives. I feel I know each and every one of them, and I'm glad to see their "fire" is blazing for all so see!

Here's hoping their fire catches or ignites yours!

Mrs. Ronnie Belanger-Carlevaro

INTRODUCTION

Not too long ago I had a heartfelt conversation over lunch with radio host and author Larry Burkett. Larry recounted his early years in business. As a young newlywed, he worked 10 hours a day, seven days a week while carrying a full-time load in school. This schedule continued for 7 years through graduate school. As a young financial executive at Cape Canaveral, Larry began his career the same way he finished school, working long hours to get ahead. A few years later his career path led him into entrepreneurship where he and a partner started a company manufacturing specialized circuit boards. As with any new venture of this kind, long hours were the norm with typical 80 hour work weeks. His skills, endurance and hard work paid off. Larry built his business to $5 million in annual sales and over 160 employees. Success! At what cost?

My story was a similar one. At the age of 23 I began my foray into business ownership with a new advertising agency and the purchase of an office building. The first few years were spent often working around the clock. As any business owner knows, these are the dues you pay for success.

Success in business, however, is not the same thing as success at home. My wife recalls the many lonely nights she spent at home with only our young daughter to keep her company. I seldom went to mid-week services at our church—it just wasn't a practical use of my time. After all, the new business required my full attention, but I was faithful to go on Sundays (even if I worked Sunday afternoons.) The lack of time with my wife created stress in our relationship.

Whenever I was home, I had quality time with my daughter. And that's what they say really counts after all, isn't it—quality, not quantity? Somehow this maxim has more rhyme than reason.

Larry's situation was more pronounced than mine. The years passed by as Larry's four children went from birth to childhood. In fact, Larry admits, there were many days in which he did not even see them. He knew them on the outside, but not on the inside.

My wife encouraged me to keep my priorities right. This meant time in prayer, time with my family, time with friends, and time at church. But there is never enough time!

She said, "If you will give your schedule over to God, He will redeem the time." In other words, if it normally takes two hours to do a project, it could now be done in one. I did not see how this could possibly work, but I gave it a try. Sure enough, as I kept my priorities, I seemed to have time for the important things, and the business prospered anyway. Instead of spending days and weeks soliciting clients, new accounts would seek me out.

This required an act of faith on my part. It caused me to rely on God's supernatural power to take over where my natural abilities left off. The act of faith requires us to set goals that are higher than we can reach—otherwise, why rely on God? This act of faith also requires humility. In effect we are confessing that God is greater than us. We are limited in our abilities and He is unlimited. For the self-made man, this simple act of faith and humility can be painfully elusive. It requires us to admit that we are not the masters of our own destiny. It is this very attitude of pride, defiance, ignorance or just plain ambivalence that keeps us from tapping into the unlimited supernatural power that is available to us!

Not only can we expect a redemption of our time when we properly order our priorities, but we can expect a greater increase in our output and freedom from the stress of always being under unyielding time demands. In other words, we have peace! Now we are working to live, not living to work! We are the master and work is the servant. When properly ordered, the work we do becomes a fulfillment of our vision, not an unyielding master.

The older I become, my definition of success changes. At one time it was measured by how much I could accumulate. Today it is measured by how much I can leave behind in the lives of others touched by someone who cared. The self-gratification of youth is no longer a goal. Now greater joy comes from giving, spending time with my children, building meaningful

relationships with friends, watching my employees prosper, serving others, and learning to love my wife in new ways.

The amazing thing about how God works in our lives is that we are not really giving up earning potential. Ordering our priorities does not come at the expense of financial prosperity. To the contrary, we will be much more likely to reach our fullest potential in every area, including income! When we are free from the emotional baggage resulting from the pursuit of money as an all-consuming goal, we can function much more effectively in every area. What we are giving up is stress, dysfunctional families, preoccupation, poor health, emotional disabilities, loneliness, greed and other unwelcome by-products. What we gain is our freedom.

The God we serve is not indifferent toward our needs. If so, then why would He have given the greatest gift—His only Son—as a sacrifice for us? Our debt was paid long ago on the Cross so we could live victorious and free today. It is abundantly clear in Scripture that God intends for us to prosper!

Many Christians labor under the misconception that riches and holiness are incompatible. Piety and poverty are not necessarily good bedfellows. In fact, one indicator of righteous living is prosperity. Just as a father delights in giving gifts to his children, so our heavenly Father does with us. The Bible is abundant with promises of gifts from God, including prosperity:

The question of how much we own is really a misnomer. All the wealth of the world, including our very bodies, belong to the Creator of the universe. We are simply stewards on a journey passing through. He has entrusted to each of us certain talents and resources. It is not the accumulation of things, but the stewardship of what we have that matters. For most of us this will require a shift in our paradigm. Real wealth can be measured in how much we give away as opposed to how much we can amass.

Life is made of choices, from the paramount to the mundane. The difference between success and failure in life is choices. Decisions made 20 years ago have consequences today. Learning how to make right choices now will determine our level of success later. Successful decision making is not learning how to guess right, but becoming skilled at the process of choosing.

God is in the business of character building. In light of eternity, the problems we face are insignificant, but how we respond to them now has eternal consequences. Problems are the pressure cookers by which our sin is exposed.

It is not talent that will bring us through a crisis—it is character. Character building is not for the faint hearted, but it precedes the success of any business. Character can be defined as what we do when no one else is looking.

All the great men of the Bible faced many hardships. This was the process of testing and refining by which their characters were shaped and molded. God is more concerned with our character than our comfort level.

The only path to this reality comes through humility. We must never forget that God is far greater than we are. The same God who molded the earth in His hands and set the stars in the heavens has the ability and resources to solve our comparatively insignificant problems.

The greatest barrier to this simple truth is our pride! As self-made men, we are used to dealing with obstacles without help from anyone. We are taught that to admit we need help is to show weakness, and no one wants to be seen as a failure. Biblical truth, however, is just the opposite. According to scriptural principles, it is when we are the weakest that we are the strongest! Why? Because only when we come to the end of our own resources will most of us humble ourselves and look to God for help. But God will only act on our behalf when we get out of the way—and He is infinitely more capable of dealing with our situation than we are.

Moving out of the realm of what we can accomplish and tapping into God's vast and limitless resources is a simple exercise of faith. What we believe about ourselves highly influences our relationship with God. What we believe about God will determine our potential in life. Either God is who He says He is, or we are wasting our time. If we don't believe what we ask for, then why ask? Part of success is living in the realm of possibilities and not circumstances—learning to see past our inability and focus on His ability.

To many, faith is simply another word for the blind suspension of reason—an excuse not to deal with our situations. In other words, faith becomes a mechanism for escape. Karl Marx said, "Faith is the opiate of the masses." Nothing could be further from the truth. It takes more faith not to believe in God!

Exercising faith also means laying down worry. Fear and faith cannot coexist. Fear is the product of unbelief. Stressful circumstances will always be with us, but allowing Him to carry our burden in the midst of trouble leads to a refreshing freedom. Faith is not an escape from storms—it is a life raft to carry us safely through the turbulence. The evidence of faith is peace in any circumstance. Now I see problems as opportunities for God to demonstrate His strength and grace. It is when I am weakest that He exercises the most power on my behalf.

Pessimists see only the problems. Optimists see the possibilities. Failure is life's greatest teacher. The most successful people in life are not those who fail the least. Successful people fail more because they try more! Winners are those who learn from their mistakes and never quit. Winners never let the obstacles in life steal their dreams. The greater the obstacles, the greater the potential! Perseverance will outlast persecution.

Through years of prosperity and failures I have learned many lessons. Chasing success following conventional wisdom was elusive, as if trying to climb a greased pole. In contrast, the principles of wisdom found in the Bible are so simple yet true. They really work! The keys to life, health, fulfillment and prosperity are all contained in Scripture. We are willing to pay thousands of dollars to listen to expensive management consultants to grasp a few nuggets of worldly wisdom when the truth is free and simple! That's what this book is all about. The stories of men who have discovered powerful truths and applied them. It's about overcoming obstacles, faith, endurance and courage. From every day lives, you will see the wisdom of biblical principles practically illustrated. Be prepared for a life-changing experience!

by Guy Carlson

Character & Integrity

Seeing is
Believing

James P Gills

SEEING IS BELIEVING

Renaissance man, Ophthalmologist James P. Gills, M.D., keeps a pace few can match.

by Brian Mast

Dr. James P. Gills has not only raced along the road of life, he has paved the streets and developed the land on either side. His secret is not the Midas touch, but rather his unwavering discipline in every area of his life. With each talent that God has given him, he has pushed himself to accomplish the maximum.

In his field of ophthalmology, he has done more cataract and lens implantation surgeries than anyone else in the world and is the founder of the internationally recognized St. Luke's Cataract and Laser Institute in Tarpon Springs, Florida. In the business arena, he owns or is the majority shareholder of approximately 30 thriving businesses, most of which are in central Florida, and has plans to develop thousands of acres he owns in his neighboring counties. In sports, he is recognized as the only person in the world to have completed six Double Iron Triathlons in less than 33 hours. He has also completed 48 marathons and 16 endurance events of 100 miles or more. He is also the co-owner of the World Triathlon Corporation that overseas many of the world's most famous triathlons. In philanthropy, Dr. Gills has given away millions of dollars and hundreds of acres to various ministries and organizations.

Achievements such as these have come about because of Dr. Gills' discipline and lifetime commitment to excellence. The rewards are abounding and awe inspiring, but the process by which he attained these goals is what makes Dr. Gills the man of character and example he is today.

Looking Back (Gills' Background)

James Pitzer Gills II was born on August 30, 1934, in Bluefield, West Virginia. From his father, a business-man, young Gills learned quickly and at the age of 13 started his own company, making clutches for motor scooters and lawn mowers and selling them across the country by mail-order. Mr. Gills instilled a hard work ethic in young "Jimmy" that has continued to this day. Jimmy learned first-hand that nothing was a hand-out as he worked hard to accomplish what he wanted. At 17 he left home to attend college and worked the summers at beaches, life-guarding and bar-tending.

He received his B.A. from Virginia Polytechnic Institute and went on to graduate from Duke University Medical School in North Carolina. He spent some time in neurology, but chose ophthalmology as his specialty. He met his future wife, Heather, the day of his graduation. After three years of dating, they were married in 1962. He went to Wilmer Ophthalmological Institute at John Hopkins University in Maryland for his Residency.

Gills returned to Duke to teach, but after three years, felt it was time to open his own practice. By specializing in ophthalmology, and more specifically in cataract surgery, he was able to treat one of the most curable causes of blindness, returning joy, hope, and independence to his patients. Prior to opening his own clinic in Florida, he operated on a man who had once been the president of an optometric association. The surgery, done to correct a difficult case of glaucoma, was so effective that the former president wrote letters of recommendation for Gills and his practice in Clearwater, Florida. Dr. Gills' clinic, opening in June of 1968, received many referrals and was successful from the very start.

Double Vision (Gills' Practice and St. Luke's)

Not Problem Free

Though Dr. Gills' practice started out on a good note, it was not without difficulties. Within a year of opening his clinic, he was maligned and scrutinized by fellow Florida ophthalmologists. His surgical technique, that of using intraocular lens implants to treat cataract patients before the procedure was perfected (such lenses were known to cause bleeding and other complications), and operating on multiple patients each day, were creating a furor among the medical community. Some ophthalmologists felt he spent less time with the patients than was adequate and acceptable in those days.

Dr. Gills' use of intraocular lens implants was considered premature by fellow doctors, but he held firm to his belief in the process. He was the first ophthalmologist in the US to limit his practice to treating cataracts via the use of intraocular lens implants, and time has proven him to be truly visionary. Today, almost all cataract surgeries in this country include the use of intraocular lenses and no doctor in the world has done more cataract surgeries with lens implantations than Dr. Gills. Fellow ophthalmologist Bob Dyer, M.D., a medical missionary with Youth With A Mission, speaks highly of Dr. Gills and says he is "probably considered to be amongst the top three most experienced eye surgeons in the world."

Finding himself a point of contention, Dr. Gills escaped the increasing pressure by relocating his practice from Clearwater to New Port Richey, just twelve miles north into the next county. When asked why he received such criticism from other ophthalmologists, Gills' response is always the same, "When you stick your head up above the crowd, somebody's going to take a swing at it." Twelve years later Gills returned, this time to straddle the northern county line with his new clinic.

In 1982, Gills formed the Cataract Teaching Foundation (CTF), which was established to assist thousands of curably blind residents in developing countries who could not afford conventional surgery. The Foundation provided inexpensive intraocular lenses and Dr. Gills trained local doctors in surgical techniques, both at St. Luke's and in other countries. Dr. Gills' cataract extraction techniques have been taught to hundreds of doctors in Central America and the Caribbean island nations. These doctors have in turn saved the sight of tens of thousands of their countrymen, many of which are children. The inevitable cycle of blindness and dependence upon others has been broken, thanks in large part to Dr. Gills' efforts.

Expansion

St. Luke's Cataract & Laser Institute opened in November of 1985 and has quite literally seen the fulfillment of a greater vision. The new clinic, a 78,000-sq ft facility has a staff of 245 (up from 140 in 1988), including 13 ophthalmologists and 7 optometrists. It has three levels with six operating rooms, family clinics, a book store, and a cafe. In 1996 alone, over 100,000 patients visited the clinic, making St. Luke's one of the largest outpatient eye surgery centers in the world.

Every patient at St. Luke's experiences the practical love of Jesus Christ. Dr. Gills and his staff share their faith by talking with patients and praying with each one before surgery. Many have been led to the Lord, which is Dr. Gills' goal. Only 50% of St. Luke's staff are Christians, however Gills likes it that way because, he says, "Iron sharpens iron." Every patient leaves knowing that Jesus is the center of what St. Luke's does.

Time Management

In the area of ophthalmology alone, Dr. Gills finds little time to sit idle. He has hosted dozens of ophthalmology seminars, published more than 140 medical articles, and authored or co-authored eight medical reference textbooks (five were best-sellers at the American Academy of Ophthalmology's annual meetings). At St. Luke's, Dr. Gills tries to maximize his time and energy.

Like his surgery procedure, Dr. Gills' office is designed for expediency. Situated in a stairwell, he is able to access patient visiting rooms and surgery suites more quickly. Since he never sits down at a desk, he reasons there is no need to have a large office. He has designed his other doctors' offices in a similar manner.

The Procedure

The average age of St. Luke's patients is 73. Each patient has an ophthalmological exam with a technician and is seen by Dr. Gills and another assistant to assess the patient's complaints. If the patient elects to have surgery that day, an ultrasound and other preoperative exams are conducted and the patient is thoroughly briefed on the procedure. Also, before the surgery, one of the staff members prays with the patient.

The process by which Dr. Gills removes the cataract (the cloudy diseased lens inside the eye) and replaces it with an intraocular lens can take only 12 minutes, but never more than a half hour. The patient feels almost nothing, due in part to the long-lasting anesthetic Dr. Gills helped introduce (topical drops, which means no needles, pain, or discomfort). Immediately after the surgery, Dr. Gills excuses himself and heads to another operating room where the same procedure will take place. The patients are then examined and sent home, with a follow-up exam the next morning. For patients from other countries, St. Luke's contacts local doctors to follow-up with them. Local referred patients return to their primary physicians.

Nothing But A Glimpse
(Gills' Sports Enthusiasm)

Not only has Dr. Gills excelled and made an impact in the medical community, he has also heavily influenced the sports world. For the avid runner, Dr. Gills has completed 48 marathons, 18 of which were Boston Marathons. For the disciplined sports enthusiast who enjoys a 2.4 mile swim, 112 mile bike ride, and a 26.2 mile run (better known as a triathlon), Dr. Gills has completed five Hawaii Ironman Triathlons and six Double Iron Triathlons. And for the extreme long-distance runners, Dr. Gills has completed 16 endurance events of 100 miles or more, and nearly 20 runs of 50 miles or more.

World Record

With the record as being the only person to have ever run six Double Iron Triathlons within the 36 hour time limit (he won the Amateur Athlete of the Year Award in 1991 after he completed five Double Iron Triathlons within the time limit,he came in 1 minute behind the first American, who was 28 years old,Gills was 56), Dr. Gills has made a meaningful and long-lasting impression upon the whole sports community. In addition, he co-owns the World Triathlon Corporation (WTC), purchased in 1991 for $3 million. The WTC oversees many of the most grueling and prestigious triathlons in the world, including the Hawaii Ironman Triathlon World Championship, and others in New Zealand, Australia, Canada, Germany, Japan, and the Canary Islands.

In July of 1996, he was honored by being asked to carry the Olympic Flame through the St. Petersburg area near his home. Several of his staff have also run marathons, triathlons, and long distance races with him, but none are as committed as he. In all his running, Dr. Gills sees himself as a participant rather than a competitor. He runs with determination, and though he may not finish first, he wins every time.

In Training

When training for races, he would run twenty three miles to work every other day. For high altitude ultra distance runs, Gills would wear a special ventilator that replicated the lack of oxygen at high altitudes. During training runs, Dr. Gills would memorize Scriptures. His wife, Heather, would often bike beside him with liquids and memory verses on cards, sometimes not giving him a drink until he had successfully memorized the verse.

Drive and Determination

In 1988 he had surgery on his left knee, which was said to have simply worn out, but Dr. Gills continued to run, bike, and swim. Though he listens to the advice of his doctors, he may not always do what they say. In 1991 he had another knee surgery, but this time because of a bicycle accident.

What drives a man to put himself through such intense training? Dr. Gills explains that his involvement in sports has enabled him to be healthy, handle stress and pressure, and to cope with his busy pace. In his book Temple Maintenance, a guide to disciplining the body, spirit, and mind, he recommends that every individual find a sport that they like and dive wholeheartedly into it. The difference it will make in their lives, he encourages, will be great and well worth the effort.

In 1996, Dr. Gills suffered a badly broken right leg in a bicycle accident and in 1998 a badly broken left leg while skiing. Both legs required multiple surgeries and has had to abandon running for now, a passion he holds very dear. If the surgeries are successful, he will be up and running again, and probably trying another Ironman if he gets his way.

Looking Into His Life (Personal and Family)

Mid-Life Crisis

The principle driving force in Dr. Gills' life, as he proclaims and as is evident in his business practices, is his relationship with Jesus Christ. When he was in his mid-thirties and just getting into his career in medicine, his life hit rock bottom. He felt like he was spiraling out of control. His family was falling apart and the daily pressures were pushing him down. He realized he was proud, ego driven, and only using God as a bail-me-out tool. His dad said to him, "Son, you won't know the Lord until you don't have anything to hold onto except Him, because you will try to do everything yourself and try to be independent until you don't have anything besides Him to hold to."

Gills had grown up with the Bible (he had read the Bible through twice by the time he was 14), but it was only head knowledge. He realized he had no real relationship with Jesus Christ and that he needed help. His marriage was less than healthy, he felt his wife was not supportive of him and his work (she too felt he wasn't supportive of her raising the children at home). He finally quit trying to do everything in his own strength with his own intelligence and committed his life to Christ.

A Change of Heart

Through prayer (a lot of it, he says) and spending time in the Word, a struggling marriage was saved and his life began to turn around. He began to run and get in shape. Shortly thereafter he ran a Boston Marathon and was forever hooked. He now says that discipline in his relationship with God and in exercise are essential in his life. Self-pity, he adds, is a harmful luxury that destroys, and though at times he would like to stay in bed, he pushes himself to keep going.

His renewed commitment to Christ took time to incorporate into his personal and professional life. He learned how to balance his day, something he continues to do, and to keep his priorities in the proper order. A typical daily schedule for Dr. Gills, even today at age 64, looks something like the following:

- up at 5:00 a.m., reading the Bible, watching Christian teaching videos, and exercising in his gym for an hour
- more exercise and at work by 6:45 a.m.
- start seeing patients at 7:00 a.m.
- in surgery from 11 a.m. until 5-7:00 p.m.
- a little golf or swimming, and home by 7-7:30 p.m.
- the rest of the evening with his wife

When it comes to taking care of his wife (something that he has had to learn), he knows the importance of spending time with her and honoring her. They try to spend each evening together and he has said the only thing that has kept him and Heather together is their faith in God and asking for His blessing on their marriage (they just celebrated their 37th wedding anniversary). Gills says that each morning he prays over Heather and blesses her from the top of her head to the bottom of her feet.

Into the Community

With both of their children grown and married, Dr. Gills and Heather have been able to play a more active role in the community. Their daughter, Shea (33), is a recent mother of 2 year old twins, a boy and a girl. She no longer practices law and is now a very happy (and busy) wife and mother. Pit, short for James Pitzer Gills III, is 29 and just graduated from the Duke University Medical Center this May and is now a Resident at University of South Florida. He too will be an ophthalmologist, with several years of residency yet to complete.

The family attends the First United Methodist Church in Tarpon Springs, Florida, where Dr. Gills is a lay leader. He frequently addresses the congregation on Sundays and speaks at other churches or social groups. Heather has just recently stopped leading a large Bible study after seven years and is now able to spend more time with Dr. Gills and her two new grandchildren.

Influential People

Dr. Gills, in a recent interview, said that the most influential person in his life was his grandmother. She had memorized the New Testament and "radiated" the joy of a relationship with Christ. He recalls how she wrote poetry and music to the Lord and spent hours singing and talking with Him.

Her example of continually communicating with Christ is a character trait that Gills shows today. He tries to integrate Christ into everything he does. His favorite Scripture says it very plainly: "I have been crucified with Christ; and it is no longer I who live, but Christ lives in me; and the life which I now live in the flesh I live by faith in the Son of God, who loved me, and delivered Himself up for me." (Gal 2:20)

Watching it Happen (Business Success)

Too Many Assets

What began as a small private ophthalmology clinic in 1968 has grown into a burgeoning conglomerate of businesses. Business was always something Dr. Gills was talented at, but he never planned to be quite this big. He says he specialized in cataract surgery "so that I could have more time, only to have that backfire as I got busier than I ever could have predicted." In 1983 he realized he needed help managing his multiple assets. He formed a company called Jireh, Inc. (a biblical name which means "the Lord will provide") in 1984, from which all of his businesses are managed and maintained. One reason for his success, Gills would say, is the fact that if you "give everything to the Lord, He will provide everything." Dr. Gills is now debt free, another blessing from the Lord.

When he first began investing in the surrounding counties, he found land to be the only option. He would pay cash for large parcels of land and was able to amass 20,000 acres. He then got into the development business by building an RV park, followed by some office buildings, apartment complexes, commercial strip centers, and a few car washes.

Impacting the Whole Community

Today, it is indisputable that Dr. Gills has profoundly and positively impacted the community. St. Luke's Cataract & Laser Institute is now the world's largest outpatient eye clinic, treating more than 100,000 patients a year. He owns the Tampa Bay Executive Airport in Pasco County, several office buildings and a billboard company called Nissi. His companies have built three golf courses and several of his larger land parcels are now successful residential real estate communities.

Gills also has his own publishing company, a ministry of St. Luke's, called Love Press. They print millions of books that are free of charge (retail value is accepted as a donation, but not required). St. Luke's is the center of all Gills' businesses, including the World Triathlon Corporation and Jireh, Inc. In all, Dr. Gills' activities employ over 400 people.

Gills' only major business loss came in the mid 1980's when much of his citrus acres were destroyed in a freeze. He held as much as 31,000 citrus acres at one time, but is now completely out of the citrus business.

Balancing Act

Managing such a broad range of businesses, while working 10 to 12 hours a day, writing books, and exercising, would seem an insurmountable task. Efficiency, business insight, and delegation play an important part in Dr. Gills' professional life. He is able to pay close attention to his businesses by carefully choosing the management staff of Jireh, Inc. His staff is responsible for overseeing the managers of each individual company. Lew Friedland, President of Jireh, Inc., has worked closely with Dr. Gills for almost fifteen years and describes Dr. Gills as having an "astute understanding of business."

During the course of each month, Dr. Gills meets with his management staff to gather information and give advice. He also meets monthly with the individual managers to discuss the activities, challenges, and expectations of each company. By spending time with the managers, he is able to make sure they perform the services as he would expect of them and to make sure his policies and wishes are carried out.

Despite the pace and magnitude of St. Luke's operations, Dr. Gills maintains that before he is a ophthalmologist, he is a care giver. When asked how he keeps it all in perspective, he said, "You are nothing but a care giver. It keeps you humble." Being a care giver is more than being a servant, "since a servant may not want to serve, but you want to serve...this is the essence of a Christian, selfless and a servant, not easy, a challenge, but very satisfying." His personal mission statement is to "care for others in the most appropriate way."

The Bottom Line

In regards to other businessmen, Dr. Gills challenges, "Be a care giver in your area of activity in the most appropriate way possible. That's what a success is, being the appropriate care giver to your people, making sure that they get the extra care and you go the extra mile. Always doing the extra thing. Do a good job first, let the bottom line take care of itself, then you can go forever." At St. Luke's they go the extra mile and offer a lot of service to their patients that other clinics don't, many for free. Dr. Gills went on to point out the difference between people. "If you're a giver, you'll be taken care of and you'll be happy. If you're a person who wants to be a receiver, you'll never be."

Dr. Gills added that a businessman needs to simply "be faithful, fervent, and focused in the thing you do best." Spending time on things that are not important was also something that Gills learned to avoid by delegating responsibility quickly.

Professional Goal

As a medical professional, he has one goal: "to survive in medicine." He struggles with the gross inadequacies of government run health care systems. He explains that in government welfare organizations, only 20% of the money, goods, or services actually makes it to the individual. The rest of the money pays for overhead and the ever increasing size of the bureaucracy. With the government's increased presence, the medical system is overloaded, he explained, and it is detrimental to the care of patients and will result in "less care, more taxes, and less medicine to minister." "All we need today," he added, "is good care. We can't even implement what we know already."

In all of his business success, Dr. Gills maintains a business principle that will last him into the next century, he views Christ as his most valuable asset.

A Sight for Sore Eyes (Philanthropy)

Daily, Dr. Gills will bring a restoration of vision that will radically restore or improve an individual's life. Many in Gills' community, most of which were never his patients, also see him as a kind and very generous man. He has donated hundreds of acres of property as locations for three new local YMCA facilities, the new campus for Trinity

Bible College, area parks, outdoor environmental "classrooms" and other worthwhile uses that will benefit the communities.

In addition to The Cataract Teaching Foundation, a non-profit organization that supports cataract surgeons in developing nations with equipment, medical supplies, and training, Dr. Gills has given millions of dollars to the numerous Christian ministries that he supports. Most of the ministries are local, but some are in India, Africa, and China. He also performs approximately 200 surgeries per year at no cost to patients who have no insurance and whose income falls below the poverty level. Dr. Gills' private foundation will outlive him and will provide funds indefinitely.

Upon his death, Dr. Gills explained that everything he has will be given to his wife, and then to a charitable trust to avoid all taxation. His desire is that everything be used for the Lord's work, since, he reasons, "We truly are only stewards while we are here."

Returning the Blessing

He has also endowed two chairs in ophthalmology, one at John Hopkins University in Baltimore (valued at $1.5 million) and one at the University of South Florida in Tampa (valued at $2 million). Both chairs were designed to fund advanced research into medical and surgical techniques to further prevent blindness.

When asked why he was so generous with his money, property, and time, he explains how little time he has on earth (how little time anyone has) and that he wants others to enjoy it now and not have to wait. His 10 inspirational books, for example, are printed at his own expense and given away free of charge. To date, over 1,000,000 have been given away, with 70% of the recipients being inmates in US prisons (St. Luke's has received thousands of letters from prisoners sharing their salvation experience or recommitment to Christ). Gills adds that he would rather give things away now and enjoy the pleasure of giving than waiting until he is dead and gone.

Seeing it to Fruition (Recognition and Awards)

Not all of Dr. Gills' hard labor has gone unnoticed. Though much of what he does daily isn't recognized or applauded by the masses, there are some things that can't be kept quiet.

Because of his business prowess and positive influence upon the communities, he was inducted into the Tampa Bay Business Hall of Fame in 1993 (the nominees were judged by twelve community leaders from the different counties).

For his ophthalmological writings, he was honored by the national publisher, Slack Inc., for writing his third best-selling ophthalmology textbook, Corneal Topography (1992 co-authored). His other two best-sellers were Small Incision Cataract Surgery (1991) and Sutureless Cataract Surgery (1990).

In 1994, he was named to Duke University Medical Center's Board of Visitors and to the Advisory Board of Wilmer Ophthalmological Institute. He was also recently named to the Board of Directors for the American College of Eye Surgeons.

His peers recently voted him to The Best Doctors in America, a prestigious publication honoring recognized medical doctors in all specialties throughout the country. In 1996 he was among the 111 Best Ophthalmologists in America selected by a national survey conducted by

Ophthalmology Times. Also in 1996, Gills received the Innovator's Award from the American Society of Cataract & Refractive Surgery, a dramatic change from the initial response he received in the late 1960's and early 1970's. This award highlights one person each year who has contributed to the development of new and innovative ideas that are changing the field of ophthalmology. About 200 guests come each year from many medical practices and centers around the country to watch Dr. Gills in surgery. He can also be found, as one would imagine, in Marquis' Who's Who in America.

Looking Onwards (To the Future)

Where can a man like Dr. Gills go after accomplishing so much in the name of Christ? The answer would undoubtably be, "Onwards." At almost 65, Dr. Gills still has much to do, as is evident by his demanding pace. He does plan to slow down a little in the near future, but that remains to be seen.

He is still meeting daily with a friend to write a textbook and an inspirational book. If Dr. Gills would pause long enough to reminisce and briefly look back over his life, he would probably discover a new area he hadn't had a chance to excel at yet, then he'd be off.

I have an idea, Dr. Gills, just keep on doing what you are doing, but leave something for the rest of us to accomplish.

Brian Mast is Editor for The Christian Businessman magazine. He can be reached at: editor@christianbusinessman.com or via the magazine's preview at www.christianbusinessman.com

More Varnish, Please

by Edwin Louis Cole

Why is it that some men require a lot of varnish to cover up their knots, cracks and bug holes, while others do not?

Real manhood is found within the heart of a man, the "inner man," his moral character, the "real man" that exudes beyond all external devices for the rest of the world to see.

Men cannot mature in moral distinctiveness with mere "head knowledge" or an "emotional catharsis," but we must constantly be evolving, purifying, changing the inner-mouse parts of our being. These inward elements create true quality in every part of life—not the exterior of a product, but the interior; not the polish on a chrome bumper, but the smooth purr of a well-tuned engine; not the talent on a ball field, but the citizenship and integrity when the spotlights go out. The quality of the inner man makes a man "real."

Shortly after WW II, I accepted a pastorate in San Bruno, California. However, only the unfinished shell of a building stood on the property. There were bare walls, a concrete floor, and old wooden benches inside. We tried to remodel the building with volunteer labor, small amounts of cash, and donated or used materials. Most of the volunteers were just that—they had little or no experience in the construction business, but wanted to give their time.

We did have a few genuine craftsmen, however. One of them was Paul, a contractor, carpenter and a craftsman of the highest degree. His woodwork was in great demand in San Francisco. During the week he built high-quality (and high-priced) houses, but he spent his Saturdays helping us complete our building.

Paul's final task was to put a wooden veneer on the wall directly behind the sanctuary's pulpit. As he labored, the rest of us were awed by the difference his exquisite work made in our building. We were proud—thrilled— that he had come to help us, and eager to tell everyone of his accomplishments. So it came as a shock when, the day Paul finished, he took me aside and asked me not to tell anyone he had done the woodwork.

"Paul, why?" I asked. "You have worked so hard and done such a beautiful thing for us! I want to tell everyone what a great job you've done"

"Please don't," he reiterated. "I'll show you why."

He proceeded to show me where the wood grain did not match exactly, where the miter was not perfectly joined, and the levels were off a fraction of an inch— things I would have never noticed if he had not pointed them out.

"I was glad to help," he said. "However, this work is not really up to my standard and I would rather not have people know I did it."

Then he hit me with it.

"I could have done a better job if the material we used had been of better quality."

I never forgot that lesson: The quality of the product depends on the quality of the material used.

Its corollary is equally true: The cheaper the merchandise, the higher the gloss. When the quality of the material is inferior, high gloss is necessary to camouflage the real product.

Furniture made from quality wood generally has only some polish to burnish it and bring out the excellence of the piece. However, furniture made from inferior woods generally has layers of lacquer or paint applied to give it a gloss that conceals the poor quality.

Knives made of tempered steel and a bone handle usually have nothing but a stamp on the blade designating the temper of the steel, and the bone is used in its natural state. However, knives made of plastic and pot metal most often have chrome on the blade and paint on the handle to give them a gloss that hides the cheap quality. The cheaper the merchandise, the higher the gloss.

> True of furniture.
> True of knives.
> True of women.
> And true of men.

Con artists, whether in the ghetto or the executive board room, are slick and sophisticated, trying to impress people with outward show to disguise their fraudulent practices.

A man of cheap character always tries to associate with, gain identity from, or control people of great talent or character. He vicariously draws upon others' identities to compensate for his own lack of integrity. Whatever he has is by association with others. Since his name is untrustworthy, he is always a name-dropper.

By contrast, the quality of the material used in becoming a "real man" results in high quality. A real man's strength of character can be relied upon. He doesn't defraud others for money, recognition, or even the respect of his family. He is real in every area of life, in every facet of his being.

Every man is limited in life by three things:

1-the knowledge in his mind,
2-the worth of his character, and
3-the principles upon which he builds his life.

These things shape a man within, for better or worse. They define the quality of his life. Quality is always internal, not external.

1. Edwin Louis Cole, *The Potential Principle* (Pitsburgh: Whitaker House, 1984).

Edwin Loius Cole is the founder and chairman of Christian Men's Network, a ministry designed to make males into men. Reprinted by permission of Thomas Nelson Publishers, Copyright© 1992, from Real Man, by Edwin Louis Cole.

Promoting
The Standard

Wes Cantrell

PROMOTING THE STANDARD

Wes Cantrell, President and CEO of Lanier Worldwide, Inc., has risen to the call of every promotion he has received—and requires the same from everyone he promotes.

by Brian Mast

Life was looking good for Wes Cantrell. He had a good job, a girlfriend and was driving a brand new 1955 Chevrolet Sport Coupe. But the comfortable life as he knew it was about to change. His new employer, Lanier Business Products, Inc., hired him as a Customer Service Representative and wanted to transfer him to Baton Rouge. "I didn't want to go," he explains, "I was still living at home. My mother was washing and cooking for me—I didn't want to destroy all that." His father, however, sided with the company. "Son, if you ever want to amount to anything, you have to go where this company wants you to go."

Young Wes listened to the words of his father, accepted the promotion and moved to Louisiana. It was a business move, he soon discovered, that would set his life on a track towards bigger success than he ever imagined possible. Cantrell quickly points out, "You know what was also waiting for me in Louisiana, Bernadine." He and Bernadine have been happily married for 42 years and are the proud parents of 4 children and 20 grandchildren. After 44 years with the business, Wes Cantrell, now the company's CEO and President, can't imagine what his life would be like if he hadn't accepted the promotion and moved away from his comfortable home town. "I look back on all that right now and realize that God had a plan," he points out, "and He guided me into it." His footsteps, it seems, were ordered from the start.

Climbing the Ladder

In 1962, Cantrell was promoted again, this time from salesman to district manager. He quickly discovered, however, "that the skills you need as a manager are totally different than those of a salesman, and I did not have those skills." The financial statistics supported his feeling—he was failing as a district manager. The profits were so marginal that there appeared to be no growth. For the first time in his life, he began to second-guess his career with Lanier.

It was during this difficult time that his wife invited him to a special meeting at their new church. That night, an evangelist named Mike Gilcrest spoke of a "Spirit-filled life." He explained that the Holy Spirit, present in someone when they become a Christian, must be given control of a person's life. He went on to say, "The Holy Spirit isn't pushy and won't run over you, but if you don't surrender to Him, you will always be frustrated and not happy as a Christian." Cantrell, 27 at the time, was tired of living life on a roller coaster—one minute high, the next minute lower than before. He wanted what the Bible calls "Life, and life more abundantly." That night, he gave up control of his will and surrendered his life to what God had for him.

Though his attitude changed, the dismal situation at work did not. The fact that business continued to fail was to him a sign that maybe he should get out of the business. But, he reasoned with himself, "I'm going to work real hard at the job I have now and give a real good day's work. If I continue to fail, I'll take it that that is God's way of guiding me into something else."

Almost immediately, business began to flourish. "Everything I touched, God caused to prosper," he explains. Cantrell knew he was in the right place at the right time and decided with renewed zeal to make the business succeed. He now admits, "I think if I had not been failing at that time, I wouldn't have heard that message." As Cantrell continually points out, "Failure is a platform for a great and rapid learning experience."

Cantrell did learn, as was evidenced by his subsequent promotions. In 1966 he moved back to Atlanta to become the Vice President and Sales Manager for dictating machine products. Then, four years later, he was promoted to Executive Vice President and National Sales Manager for all Lanier diction products and 3M copier products, including the newly created International Division. In 1972 he was elected to the board of Lanier's former parent company, Oxford Industries. Five years later, he was named President of Lanier Business Products, Inc. Lanier was spun off from Oxford Industries at that time and traded on the New York Stock Exchange. Then, in 1983, the business was acquired by Harris Corporation, which in time named Cantrell the President and Chief Executive Officer of Harris/3M Document Products, Inc., a joint-venture between Harris and the 3M Company. In 1989, he was elected an officer of Harris Corporation and became President and CEO of Lanier Worldwide, Inc. (renamed in 1990 when Harris bought 3M's interest in the venture).

After looking at Cantrell's promotion record, he may need to view failure not as a platform, but rather a springboard for a great and rapid learning experience.

Successful Management

Becoming a District Manager was a pivotal decision, but deciding to be the best manager possible was a life-changing experience, for him and virtually thousands of other Lanier employees. As a manager, and eventually CEO and President of the company, he is highly influential in the promoting and positioning of individuals within Lanier Worldwide. He sees his position as a place of honor and responsibility, with the primary focus of fitting the right people into the right job. He prayerfully considers individuals for promotion and transfer, but is careful not to push them into an undesired position. Many years ago, he admits, "I would say, in a nice way, 'You know, you really need to go to Los Angeles, or else it is going to be all over for you career wise.'"

He has learned to be more sensitive towards those who work with him. Tom McElheny, President of CPN (Christian Purchasing Network), the largest purchaser of Lanier copiers, has known Cantrell for many years. He describes Cantrell as being "warm, tough, loyal, caring, and filled with integrity. In short, the kind of man another would value as a friend, counselor, business partner or fishing buddy." Such comments are not uncommon. McElheny works closely with Lance Herrin, General Manager of Lanier Office Systems, and says, "For six years Lance and his staff have spoken with consistent respect/ affection towards Wes."

Today, management has taken on a whole new meaning. Under Cantrell are seven Executives within Lanier who themselves manage thousands of people and are responsible for billions of dollars in sales. Managing, it turns out, is an area in which Cantrell has excelled, in every sense of the word. McElheny adds, "Wes serves as both a personal and business standard from which his colleagues may judge or measure their personal actions and decisions." Larry Burkett, President of Christian Financial Concepts and long-time friend and confidant of Cantrell, when asked what has been the deciding factor in Cantrell's success, simply said, "Quality leadership." It is no wonder why Lanier Worldwide has continued to increase.

In 1997, net income was up 17 percent and sales were up five percent. In fact, as Lanier's monthly summary reports, the improvement occurred in virtually every geographic area around the world. For Lanier, which has 1,600 sales and service centers located in 100 countries and employs 5,845 people in the US and 2,242 overseas, such a worldwide increase is on a grand scale.

Foundational Principles

Not all of Cantrell's learning came from on-the-job training. He credits his father, who worked as a minister, a schoolteacher and a principal of an elementary school, with much of it. His father, he says, "was a deeply spiritual father who practiced what he preached." He always acted, spoke and worked in a manner that demanded respect. Perhaps the greatest influence, Cantrell fondly recalls, was that "he didn't have a double standard." As a result, young Cantrell grew up with similarly strong convictions.

Then, when Cantrell was only 15 years old, these beliefs were severely tested. His father was unexpectedly fired from the church he pastored. "As a 15-year-old boy, that made me very angry," Cantrell recalls. But his father, even more unexpectedly, chose to forgive those who offended him and returned to the church as a Sunday school teacher, all the while treating the new pastor with respect and dignity. Later, his father became a substitute preacher and was eventually asked to pastor another church in the area. Young Cantrell learned first-hand what it meant to be submissive and humble, and adds, "It made a profound impact on my life."

The effect was long lasting. In every position he had over the years at Lanier, he made the effort to be the best and excel in that specific area. Promotions followed, not because he sought them, but because he showed himself capable and faithful. His personal mission statement, not surprisingly, is a mirror of his actions. In brief, he believes "a good name is rather to be chosen than great riches" (Proverbs 22:1). A good name, he points out, means being in right relationship with God, his wife, his family and his business, in that order. The result, he explains, "is that you know and obey Christ, your wife trusts you (what you tell her is true and you never mislead or manipulate her), and so on, down to your children and then to your business associates and your customers." He takes his mission statement seriously, and his life reflects it, much to the pleasure of those around him.

Beating the Odds—Again

Then, in August of 1996, Cantrell's fast-paced business world came to a stop. During a routine physical, he was told he may have prostate cancer. The results from the biopsy were positive. "It was a devastating experience," he says candidly, and adds, "Right away I was very emotional and having a pity party. I was saying, 'I've been a good boy, Lord, why are you letting this happen to me?'" Cantrell soon realized that he could not afford to indulge in self pity, but rather "get back to what I believed to be true." He began studying the Bible with renewed vigor to see what God had to say on the matter.

34

It was not long before he found his answer. While reading and praying, he found what God was saying to him in Job 5:25-27: 1) your offspring shall be as the grass of the earth, 2) you shall live to a ripe old age, and 3) be sure this is for your good. Now, he says, "When I wake up, I think of those Scriptures." The bottom line, he now states boldly, is that "I am not going to die without His permission. I am not going to die out of His timing."

Almost immediately after hearing the biopsy results, the entire family came together in the Cantrell home. For two hours they discussed the situation, resulting in the suggestion from his children that he not do anything until the Lord let him know what to do. The family also agreed to fast together the next weekend. Then they gathered around Cantrell and prayed for him. He began to seek counsel and advice from other people, reading and seeking information. One of the first people he called for counsel was well-known author and radio host Larry Burkett, who had been diagnosed with cancer about two years before. Today, as part of the ongoing treatment, Cantrell drinks lots of pure water, maintains a vegan diet and takes plenty of herbs and supplements. As a result, his PSA (see text box on facing page) levels have dropped from the first biopsy's 4.7 to a substantially lower 3.6. Such a decrease is a good sign, and Cantrell is pleased. He candidly explains, "There are many good things that came out of having prostate cancer, but the main one is that it has driven me to a deeper trust and reliance on the Lord." Which, he admits, is definitely for his good.

As for retirement, Harris Corporation has a mandatory retirement policy at age 65 for Senior Executives.

Cantrell, now 64, will sidestep retirement when he becomes Chairman of the Board at Lanier, which is poised to become a new independent company under the same name.

Cantrell says the spin-off will position Lanier to compete more effectively in both office equipment sales and the investment community. Harris, in turn, will streamline operations and focus purely on the communications industry.

Lanier Worldwide plans to be open for public trade and will apply for listing on the New York Stock Exchange. "We are extremely excited about the opportunity to become a public company," Cantrell says, not to mention the fact that retirement will no longer be mandatory. The spin-off is expected to be finalized by the end of the summer, 1999.

As Cantrell remains with Lanier, thousands of customers and employees will continue to be impacted by his dedication to service with excellence. Maybe now Cantrell can raise the standard even higher.

GETTING THE PERSON RIGHT

by Zig Ziglar

In selling, when we get the "person" right, it's easier to get the "salesperson" right.

"The most important discovery of our time is the realization that we can alter our lives by altering our attitudes."

Some of you are able to identify with the busy executive who came home with a briefcase full of work. His six-year-old son was demanding time, but due to deadlines, the father reluctantly told the boy he had several hours of work that took priority. The lad asked this recurring question, "Can't you play now, Dad?" The young salesman had a brilliant idea. Before him was a newspaper containing a map of the world. He tore the paper in pieces and gave it to his son to put back together, telling him that when the "puzzle" was finished, there would be time to play together. The salesman bargained for some uninterrupted time. However, in a matter of minutes the youngster called his dad to look at the map. Astonished the father asked how he had managed to do it so quickly. The youngster explained that on the other side of the map was a picture of a man and that once he got the man right, the world was right.

Getting the Person Right

In selling, when we get the "person" right, it's easier to get the "salesperson" right. The "secret" to getting YOU right is getting your "attitude" right. Of all the occupations, the sales profession is the most demanding as far as maintaining the right mental attitude is concerned. In sales, we seek our prospects, and many times our calls come at inopportune times and are often made on people who are not always excited about seeing us. When you add the fact that many do not feel a need or have an interest in what we are selling, and the stage is set for a fairly high "turndown" rate for discussing our goods and services-much less for doing a full presentation. When this process is repeated a number of times each day, the salesperson runs the risk of having the ego damaged.

There is no way you can build an armored shell to totally protect against feelings of frustration, disappointment, and fear. If you could, you would NOT be a very successful salesperson. The same "feelings" that lead to excitement lead to disappointment. Since we are not immune to "down" feelings, the question is, What can we do to limit their frequency, length, and severity? Taking control is important because our attitude determines how many calls we make, when we start, how we finish, and the results we obtain each day.

You Don't Miss It Until It's Gone

Health is one of those things we become enormously concerned about when there is a possibility we're going to lose it—and yet we take it for granted while we have it. The most significant aspect of a career in selling is a salesperson's health. Consider the following "stressors" affecting your health: the need to meet quotas, introduction of new products, increased competitiveness for the consumer dollar, high-tech aspects of the business, increased emphasis on customer service and quality products, and traffic congestion. These "distress items" place pressure—physical, mental, and spiritual—on the salesperson. How can you take care of yourself in this climate? Mankind is tri-dimensional: physical, mental and emotional (spiritual). The answer lies in evaluating yourself in these three areas.

Protecting Your Physical Health

In the quest for the right attitude, physical health is a key component. This area is neglected by most salespeople. Taking care of your health will pay dividends in increased energy and fewer days spent in sickness. Your extra energy will produce increased revenue for your family. The most important key to taking care of your physical health is discipline. When you discipline yourself to do the things you need to do when you need to do them, the day will come when you can do the things you want to do when you want to do them." Consider this: If you start your day in the proper manner, it sets the "tone" for the entire day.

Several times each week you need to choose an activity that causes your heartbeat to be accelerated into the "target range" recommended by your physician and keep your heart working for a certain number of minutes (Ask your doctor to tell you what your "target range" for exercise is. Your doctor can also help you choose an activity that will fit your personality and life-style). To maintain your fitness level, work out three times per week; for minimal changes over time, work out four times per week; for maximum changes in fitness, work toward working out five times per week. This exercise schedule can aide in controlling weight, reducing stress, lowering cholesterol and blood pressure, not to mention what it does for maintaining your energy level.

Remember, exercise is not something you spend time doing, it's something you invest time in. When you are physiologically energized and psychologically confident, you've added two powerful ingredients to your way of life and approach to selling. Being healthy physiologically and psychologically will enable you to focus on the things going right instead of the things going wrong. I encourage you to think about your health before you have placed yourself in jeopardy!

The benefits to getting the person right and then getting the salesperson right are astronomical. Go out and establish the habits that will allow you to maintain the proper attitude for the healthy and successful life you deserve to live!

Zig Ziglar is one of the most sought after motivational speakers in the country and a best selling author. Reprinted by permission of Thomas Nelson Publishers. From the book Ziglar on Selling. Copyright © 1991, Zig Ziglar

Major Among Men

Men

Edwin Louis Cole

Major Among Men

The Standard for Manhood is as follows: Manhood and Christlikeness are synonymous.

by Brian Mast

These words resound in the ears of millions of men around the world. Words of truth, once spoken, have a way of piercing hearts and minds. What they hear is simple, yet packed with explosive power. If men are to accept the above statement as true, then certain unavoidable repercussions will follow. These repercussions are exactly what Edwin Louis Cole, President of Christian Men's Network, expects.

Repercussions ...

Men need "to be taught to accept responsibility," Cole boldly proclaims, and adds, "Maturity is accepting responsibility." Being responsible means keeping your word and thereby becoming a man of integrity. Such men will view their word as their bond.

For men who want to be successful fathers, he continually says, "Accept the call—be the man (father) of the home." Children have four core needs: intimacy, discipline, love and value. These four are the ingredients for normalcy, he explains, and MUST be met at home. If not, children will seek it elsewhere and may "fail in school or adopt a surrogate father." Until this generation of men get a revelation of the importance and impact a father can have on his offspring, the children of today will grow up to be the ill-equipped adults of tomorrow. After all, kids won't always listen to you, but they will always imitate you.

In regards to men treating their wives, Cole has a lot to say. Men are to "guide, guard, govern, to direct, protect, correct, to nourish, cherish, admonish," a pattern that is consistent with God's Word and example. He encourages men to treat their wives as joint heirs or, he says, according to I Peter 3:7, "your prayers won't be answered." A man's life is summed up in three words: stewardship, relationship, and leadership. Money and sex, he adds, "are of God, for loving and giving, not lusting and getting."

Get Real

Ed Cole has walked the road of hard knocks enough to know firsthand what men need at their core. He grew up in a "divided house," he explains, with a mother who regularly prayed for him and a father who would get violent when drunk. Once, after an altercation, young Cole purposed one thing: to some day out drink his father. Much of his high school years, he admits, were spent learning how to drink.

One night, however, he arrived at a party to find his dad already passed out. He suddenly realized the glaring truth: "Dad was wrong and Mom was right." Young Cole didn't change immediately, but he says, "I followed my dad's pattern, but I couldn't outrun my mother's prayers." Cole's father eventually made his peace with God, though just four days before his death.

After a stint in the Armed Services, during which he fell in love with and married Nancy, he got a job and began to do "the typical thing." Nonetheless, he found that he couldn't escape what he remembered as a child. Finally, he admitted the emptiness in his heart could only be filled in one way. He cried out, "God, here

I am, forgive me." The response to God's forgiveness was immediate. "I was so full of joy," he explains. "I witnessed to everyone about it and preached everywhere."

Nancy, however, was not too impressed with Cole's newly found faith. About 3 years later, when Nancy was pregnant with their first child, they both got down on their knees and prayed that they would be united in their beliefs. In time, she began to read the Bible more and more, eventually understanding that "the just shall live by faith" (Romans 1:17). She accepted the Lord soon after, as have all of their children: Paul, Joann and Lois. They have been married now for 53 years.

Why Men?

For over 20 years Ed Cole has traveled the globe, challenging men in different cultures and nations to do one thing: be a man. His message, like the need around the world, does not change. It is imperative, he explains, that men rise up and take spiritual authority in their homes and families. The absence of fathers has resulted in staggering statistics of drug abuse, teen pregnancies and acts of violence among youth. Today, nearly 40 percent of all American children do not live with their fathers as a result of divorce or unwed childbearing.[1] The effect is observable: 60 percent of America's rapists, 72 percent of adolescent murderers, and 70 percent of juveniles in state reform institutions grew up without a father.[2]

Cole's ministry to men began to crystallize in the mid 1970s. As a pastor, he often had the opportunity to speak to men, but it wasn't until one night in a small church in Oregon did he understand his calling. God gave him a prophetic word that proved to be powerful

45

and life changing. Without God's help, Cole says, the meeting would have been a flop. Instead, it was a tremendous event where men began to stand up and take responsibility for their actions, and history was made. He left the event overflowing with excitement and vision, fully planning to impact the world. The plan has not changed over the years. If anything, it has increased ten-fold.

According to Ben Kinchlow, long-time friend of over 25 years and former co-host on the 700 Club, "Ed Cole is the father of today's men's movement." The key to Cole's ongoing success, Kinchlow explains, is "his commitment to obey and faithfully teach the principles of God's Word without compromise."

Since 1980, when Cole formed Christian Men's Network (CMN), he has challenged men in 115 nations. While the CMN Saturday events reach about 35,000 to 40,000 people each year, their video series reach hundreds of thousands around the world. CMN now has offices in 17 countries and has plans to minister in 210 nations by the year 2001. The men's movement is expanding more rapidly overseas than in the US, Cole explains, "because they want it." In June of 1997, CMN's International Communication Center was completed. This training facility now acts as a launching pad for hundreds of men who will in turn impact other nations.

Men everywhere are rising up and "becoming a man." Recently, a woman in Texas gave a copy of Cole's book, Maximized Manhood, to her brother-in-law. He started reading it and that Sunday went to church for the first time in years. He literally ran forward to ask Christ into his heart. Between the time of him getting the book and going to church, he had visited his ex-girlfriend and apologized for the way he treated her. He explained, "Now I know how to be a man and how to treat a woman." The change in his life was instantaneous.

Similarly, Janno Peensalu, born in Estonia during communist rule, had his life greatly impacted by the message of Ed Cole. Three months after accepting Christ in an underground church, young Janno (then age 18) heard Cole's message on manhood and felt compelled to offer the same message to his fellow Estonians. He began to translate Maximized Manhood at the slow pace, he explains, "of half a page per day." In the process of translating the book and listening to Cole's videos, Janno learned English. Today, at the age of 27, Janno is a leader of the men's movement in his nation and is pastor of a growing church in Estonia.

The travels of Ed Cole have impacted the globe, changing the course of history for hundreds of thousands of men. Cole, however, is the first to explain, "It would have been wrong of the donkey that carried Jesus into Jerusalem to think that the fan-fare was for him." What he means, in his own candid way, is that all the credit, praise and thanks belong solely to God. Anything else would be out of place.

INTEGRITY IN THE MARKETPLACE

by Pastor George A. Brantley

If You Don't Have Integrity,
You Don't Have Anything

What do you do when no one else is looking? What do you watch on TV when you're on a business trip? When you are traveling alone, what kinds of magazines do you browse through while waiting for your connecting flight? The answers to these and other similar questions can quickly reveal the level of integrity in a man's heart. Why? Because your integrity can be defined by who you are when only God is watching.

Like many of us, King David was a man who blew it. Of that there is little doubt. However, David always fell to his knees and repented to his Father when the error of his ways was revealed. I believe the only reason King David is in the kingdom of heaven and "right" with God today is because he was a man whose heart was after God. And, like King David, we will reveal our hearts through the nature of our repentance. The first part of 1 Kings 9 makes it plain:

> And it came to pass, when Solomon had finished building the house of the Lord and the King's house, and all Solomon's desire which he wanted to do, that the Lord appeared to Solomon the second time

as He had appeared to him at Gibeon. And the Lord said to him, "I have heard your prayer and your supplication that you have made before Me; I have consecrated this house which you have built to put my name there foreve and My eyes and My heart will be there perpetually. Now, if you walk before me as your father David walked, in integrity of heart and in uprightness, to do according to all that I have commanded you, and if you keep My statutes and My judgments, then I will establish the throne of your kingdom over Israel forever."

This scripture reveals that our Lord honored the integrity in King David's heart by establishing his throne forever. Like David, we must desire that God establish our throne (home) forever. When we leave this earth our integrity will determine the legacy of our name. Through doing all that God has set before us, by walking upright in purity before the Lord in holiness and by being men of righteousness in everything we do, God will prove Himself faithful by establishing our name in the lives of our children and our children's children forever.

Those without integrity fool themselves into believing no one is watching and their sin is undetected. However, the truth remains that the only One who truly matters is always watching. He never sleeps or walks far enough away that our sin becomes hazy in the distance. Everything we do throughout our lives is observed by God.

The Vitality of Integrity

Nothing is more vital than integrity of the heart. Eternal security and assurance of our salvation will come through searching our hearts. If our hearts expose a lack of integrity, we must turn to God and repent. We cannot ignore what seems like "just a little sin" because little sins, like a claw around our neck, will grow and ultimately choke the very life out of us. We must deal with every sin regardless of how we perceive its magnitude.

The bottom line before God and man is our integrity—that is all we have. From our integrity comes our name, which is in turn broadcast to the world. Everything we possess, from our car to our home to the clothes we wear, is like dust that will one day float away and disappear. Every material possession is nothing, but our name (our integrity) is everything.

It doesn't matter how many little fish logos we have on the back of our cars, on our business cards, or in our yellow page ads. If our name is not worthy of honor out in the world, we are not honorable. In reality, many people view the Christian fish logo as a warning sign, prompting them to look elsewhere. This is because many so-called "Christian" brothers have sacrificed integrity for a "fast buck" and now have names that are not worthy of honor.

When we choose to be men of integrity, even the ungodly will show us favor. God will go before us on our behalf and give us favor with those who would otherwise not patronize our businesses.

I believe with all my heart that a businessman who is in the church but lacks integrity is a reproach to God's kingdom. Most pastors, I am certain, would agree that it would be better for such a man not to tell people he is a Christian or even attends church until he gets his life in order. Whether we like it or not, our name represents all that is good or corrupt about our lives.

A recent Gallop poll showed that only 18% of the American people believe that business executives have high or very high ethical standards. What an opportunity for Christian businessmen in today's market, and as God opens doors, their light will naturally shine before all men.

Enough is never enough

I believe God does not require us to "kill" ourselves in order to succeed in business. Contrary to popular opinion, neglecting all else and working 2, 3 and 4 jobs for the sake of success is not Godly. When we line our lives up with truth and prioritize our time, God will go before us and make our crooked paths straight. That is why the Word says the steps of a righteous man are ordered of the Lord. Through hard work, integrity and faithfulness, God will be glorified in our lives and thus reward us with the righteous desires of our hearts.

By the same token, the degree of integrity we exhibit in our own lives will be reflected in how we bless those who work for us in our businesses. We cannot expect our employees to work diligently when they have no faith in our integrity or our ability to take care of them. The old adage holds true: "You get what you pay for." Consequently, while working for someone else, we should work hard and allow God to take care of our needs. In short, we need to let promotion come not from our "wheeling and dealing," but from God.

While God directing our steps, we need to always remember to glorify God in all we do. As Philippians 2:12 says, "Therefore, my beloved, as you have always obeyed, not as in my presence only, but now much more in my absence, work out your own salvation with fear and trembling; for it is God who works in you both to will and to do for His good pleasure. Do all things without complaining."

Through this timeless principle of glorifying God, a man's name can impact those around him in the market place. Is your name impacting the world around you? Remember, you are the created of God. We must never underestimate our uniqueness in God. What does your name say in the market place? Does your name represent a life lived above reproach? Is your name spoken among those who are faithful to work in balance and diligence? You are a special person that God created for such a time as this. God placed you exactly where you are meant to be, doing what He has called you to do.

In addition, we need to give ourselves to what we are doing in the degree it takes to become the very best. 1 Chronicles 12 says, "they were skilled with the right hand and they were skilled with the left hand".

To me, this means that if you sell, decide what it takes to be the best salesman without being a liar or a cheat. Your life should redefine who a salesman is, and those who know you should not fear being around you. You can, and should, live such a life of integrity that a finger can never be pointed at you as a reproach to the Kingdom of God.

If you sell shoes, don't sell your customers the most expensive shoes, but rather the best shoes for their needs. If you sell cars, sell your buyers what they need, not the highest price car on the lot because you need the commission. Leave your commission (your provision) to God. If you are a home builder, build a house that is above reproach. If you are a doctor, give the best treatment you can and become a doctor of righteousness. If you are an attorney, redefine what it means to be an attorney.

God wants to move in every man's life who will choose the way of integrity. When we get our lives in order and lined up with truth, there will come a time and a season when the blessings of God will literally overtake us from behind.

I challenge you to choose life, choose truth, choose the blessing of God and walk as a man of integrity.

George A. Brantley is the founder and Senior Pastor of The Rock of Gainesville, Florida, a dynamic and relevant church to this generation.

BUSINESS OPPORTUNITIES & REALITY CHECKS

by A L Andrews

Reality checks don't bounce.
Make sure your opportunity is backed with reality

Every day we are being bombarded with an abundance of "opportunities." An opportunity is "a combination of circumstances favorable for the purpose," according to Webster's New World Dictionary. Regardless how good it looks and how well others have done with it, the important question to ask is, "Is this opportunity really one for me?"

Proverbs 19:21 says, "Many are the plans in a man's heart, but it is the Lord's purpose that prevails." The only thing that will prevail or truly endure and produce in our lives is what the Lord has purposed for us. The Word of God says that He has plans for us (Jeremiah 29:11) and that those plans are to prosper us. It would be a mistake to assume, just because an opportunity looks good, has worked for others, and is available, that it must be OK for us.

Just because something works for someone else does not guarantee that it will work for you. David, while he was yet a boy, set an example for us. When King Saul was ready to release him to go after Goliath, he placed his tunic and armor on David. Because David was not used to them, he decided he could not use them. It turned out to be the right decision. David took his own tools, a staff and a sling, because he knew these tools and was skilled with them. While the King's armor worked for Saul, David's equipment worked for him and got him the victory he was believing for.

All too often, individuals jump into opportunities to invest precious resources—time, money, talent—only to be gravely disappointed and even suffer severe losses when it does not work out as anticipated. What worked at another time, in another place, and for someone else may not work for you at this time for many reasons. Here are just a few:

1. The conditions you are dealing with are not exactly the same; The talents & abilities God developed within you can't be effectively applied this way:

2. God's purpose for you may actually take you along a different path;

3. Doing what the world has done doesn't always produce God's intended results; and

4. The validity of the opportunity may last only a short time because it was fad-driven.

This does not mean that we don't look at the success (or lack of it) others have had when we are making our decisions. It is to our advantage to observe the results others may or may not be getting to determine if something could be feasible for us. We can learn much about how to approach certain options to gain the best results (and should always be ready to learn) from others mistakes and successes as well as our own. "Any enterprise is built by wise planning, becomes strong through common sense, and profits wonderfully by keeping abreast of the facts" (Proverbs 24:3-4, TLB).

There are a few general, common sense principles that you should apply to help determine whether any investment is wise for you. Though these concepts are basic and widely known, you would be amazed how often people overlook them.

1. "Everything that glitters isn't gold." Every deal you will be presented with is usually packaged in its Sunday best. Only with diligent investigation can you be sure of what you may be getting. Some of the best sources of information will be others in the same business. They can tell you a lot about the pitfalls and rewards, since they have uncovered them personally. If you can't find out enough to make a valid decision, it is better to pass it up." (Proverbs 21:16).

2. "Don't start something you can't afford to finish." Every business requires more resources than the basic costs of the business (rent, utilities, merchandise, purchase price [if buying]). There are a myriad of costs that many folks never think of until they meet them face-to-face after starting-up. Be sure that you have reviewed every possible cost, including the initial investment. Then look honestly at your resources to be sure you have more than enough to get the business really established (Luke 14:28-30).

3. "If it looks too good to be true, it probably is." If, after looking into the venture and asking all the questions, all you see is the "Sunday best" and you haven't uncovered any down side, then walk away. No business venture is without risk. If that were true, everybody would be wanting in and everyone would be making millions of dollars. The fact that something has a down-side or risks does not make it unfavorable. Not knowing what these are, is what will get you in trouble." (Proverbs 23:4)

4. "Never invest in an arena you don't know a lot about." Eager to get into business for themselves, many people have bought into ventures that they really know little or nothing about. Many of these have had disastrous results. With all the demands of business, nobody needs to be playing catch-up on how the business works. Additionally, how can you ever do a valid evaluation unless you know what you are looking at. Every industry has its own peculiarities, hidden hazards and set of risks. Unless you are very familiar with the industry, it will be basically impossible for you to assess the value of the business to you or to know how to make it successful." (Proverbs 24:5)

4 Biblically based steps to apply

#1. Explore all the factors: It is rare when you can, at the first look, see the real potential and associated risks of an opportunity. Spend all the time necessary to get all the facts. before jumping into anything. There are often many "hidden" factors and costs that are left up to you to uncover. "A simple man believes anything, but a prudent man gives thought to his steps" (Proverbs 14:15).

#2. Evaluate your data: Review the facts you gather to determine if there is really an opportunity for you. Will it really make the profit needed? Can it produce enough to justify the investment? Is there a real market. "Every prudent man acts out of knowledge, but a fool exposes his folly" (Proverbs 13:16).

#3. Educate yourself: No matter how good the opportunity, you will never be able to make the most of it unless you are prepared. Get all the "how to" training and information you can. The more prepared you are the more likely your prospects for success. "Apply your heart to instruction and your ears to words of knowledge" (Proverbs 23:12).

#4. Execute a definite plan: Without a well thought out plan to direct you specifically, you can get off course and lose the very advantage you expected to achieve from the opportunity. An effective plan will let you take hold of the opportunity. "The plans of the diligent lead to profit as surely as haste leads to poverty" (Proverbs 21:5).

While this is being mentioned last, the first thing you should do is PRAY. Seek God early on, all during your evaluation process, and before your final decision. Never be in too much of a hurry to wait until you know you have God's direction on it. Proverbs 3:5-6 says it this way,

"Trust in the Lord with all your heart and lean not on your own understanding; in all your ways acknowledge him, and he will make your paths straight" and James 1:5 says, "If any of you lacks wisdom, he should ask God, who gives generously to all without finding fault, and it will be given to him."

Go take hold of those opportunities!

A. L. Andrews in an author, seminar speaker and small business consultant. He is the founder of Building on the Rock Ministries. Each of these organizations are dedicated to "Helping to build thriving businesses—God's way." Contact him at CEO@tceonline.com or www.tceonline.com

Power Point

by Bob Harrison

"Crisis does not develop character,
but reveals it." —Jess Gibson

Toilet Paper puts a squeeze on principal

What character traits do you need to focus on in order to make your private life consistent with your public life? What are your deep-down-in-the-heart values?

Police used a marked roll of toilet paper to catch a principal who was stealing bathroom tissue from his school. The markings, which could only be seen under ultraviolet light, were put on the paper by the police after a school janitor reported that he noticed rolls were routinely missing from a supply room after the principal ate his lunches there.

Here is an example of a person who went through intensive training and preparation to obtain a position of leadership, only to see his career go "down the drain." As with many others, while succeeding in academic training, he apparently failed in character training.

The dictionary defines character as distinctive traits or behaviors that is typical of a person.

Character is a learned behavior. It is best taught at a young age by precept and example at home, as illustrated by . . .

Jess Gibson

Jess Gibson is an incredible motivational speaker, pastor, and friend from Springfield, Missouri. Here we'll see him share one of his tests of character as a young boy:

"At the age of fifteen, I had a before-school job at a pharmacy. One morning I was sweeping behind the counter where the cash register sat. All of a sudden I saw it.

"A beautiful crisp $10 bill was laying there, just waiting for me to pick it up. The boss was in the basement. No one else was in the store. Who would know? Should I, or shouldn't I?

"What could I do with $10? Visions of candy and sugar plums danced through my head! Then it dawned on me. My trustworthiness, my character was being tested. My actions at that precise moment would shed light on who I really was and who I could become.

"I picked up the money, ran to the basement, and presented it proudly to the owner. He didn't even say thanks, but grumbled that someone had been clumsy handling money.

"However, I had my reward in that this experience revealed to me that I had developed the character traits that would guide me throughout life, and enable me to overcome bigger challenges and temptations."

Each action you take when faced with moral questions or temptations will help form your habits, which in turn will determine your character.

But (we) have renounced the hidden things of dishonesty . . . commending ourselves to every man's conscience in the sight of God.
—2 Corinthians 4:2

Bob Harrison is President and Founder of International Christian Business Leaders and Harrison Internaitonal Seminars, both headquartered in Tulsa, Oklahoma. By combining his financial background with his biblical training, he brings forth a powerful anointing that causes financial miracles. His valuable material has been shared with thousands of businesses, corporations, and seminar groups with audiences up to 25,000.

Used with permission from Power Points for Success, by Bob Harrison. Copyright 1997, Honor Books Publishers.

Investing Biblical Principles

Investing is Not an Option Play

Darrin Smith

INVESTING IS NOT AN OPTION PLAY

Saving for the future may seem defensive, but Darrin Smith, linebacker for the Seattle Seahawks, has found it to be the best offense

by Brian Mast

For boxing great Joe Louis, his incredible dream became a financial nightmare. His battle with the IRS is public knowledge, as is the fact that he gave much of his money away, including an entire earning from one fight ($65,200, about $700,000 in today's money) to World War II efforts. But when all was said and done, Joe Louis didn't retire comfortably (He even came out of retirement in an attempt pay some of his back-taxes.), he died poor and in debt.

Such is the common challenge for many sports heroes of today. The pay, bonuses, endorsements, and perks last only as long as these individuals can perform. They know that hundreds of "wanna be heroes" are jockeying for their position and pay rate. A sudden injury could mean the end of the road, literally, for many of these professional athletes.

And all the while, taxes are due and great investing "opportunities" are available at every turn. These pressures, combined with the often abundant amount of money, is a dangerous combination. "I've heard the tragic stories of men who had it all, but ended up with nothing," says Darrin Smith, linebacker for the Seattle Seahawks, "and some of these guys are on the streets today.

Agent of Change

Instead of getting angry at the system, Darrin, who has been playing pro football since 1993, decided to do something about it.

He used his MBA degree that he received from the University of Miami, where he played football for then-coach Jimmy Johnson, and investment experience to co-found IAOBM, the International Association of Black Millionaires. Darrin's partner, Michael Chatman, was a motivational speaker and businessman, and their combined talent and vision marked the beginning of an organization that focused on helping black professionals not only keep but also increase the finances they presently have.

The basis behind individuals losing everything, according to Darrin, "is a factor of poor planning and poor preparation." The bottom line goal of IAOBM is to provide the planning and preparation necessary so that individuals and their families will be taken care of when the short-term business opportunity (i.e. football) is finished. "Our business does not last long," Darrin admits, "so you have to plan and maximize the opportunity when it presents itself."

"I have always been a planner," he says, which was why he was able to condense a 6-year MBA degree into 5 years, while at the same time playing college football. During his senior year, he interned at a financial institution and gained practical investment knowledge, which enabled him see first hand the benefits of investing.

After listening to a lot of locker room talk and seeing the challenges that players faced, Darrin began to get a sense for something he could do. In addition, many of the rookies on the team would approach him and ask for insight on their investment opportunities. Darrin says with smile, "Sometimes I would say, 'Don't buy the exotic ostriches right now, focus on a more simple and steady investment.'" With countless people pestering the players with, "Hey, I have a plan for you," Darrin's rational advice couldn't have come at a better time. The need for education was evident, Darrin explains, "so forming IAOBM was a natural option for me."

What exactly is the International Association of Black Millionaires and how does it help its members? The name is an eyecatcher, Darrin admits, but being a millionaire is not a requirement. In fact, the desire to change is far more important. "We want our members to dream and to become successful," he points out, "so what you start with is not near as important as what you end up with."

To reach this goal, IAOBM offers a variety of resources to its members. One of the primary benefits that has the biggest impact on the members is the network that is formed. Darrin explains, "One member, who might be a dentist in California, can call a fellow member in Florida and ask for advice about setting up a private practice."

Once a year members meet for a weekend of special financial training, during which certain members speak on such relevant topics as asset protection and estate planning. This increases the individual's business as well as encourages networking among those in attendance. Growth among businesses through IAOBM is targeted, but preparation for future growth through training, education and networking is always a principal focus.

Different levels of membership exist, and even among members, some are more involved than others.

What an individual gets out of IAOBM is always subject to a person's degree of involvement, but Darrin always desires for the maximum impact. Membership is not free, but for those who can't afford the fee, Darrin makes sure that audio tapes and books are made available.

When it comes to making an investment, Darrin makes it clear, "The individuals do all the investing themselves, we simply educate and inform." IAOBM is not a get-rich-quick scheme, but rather it is all about exposure to the options and basic fundamentals of investing.

Though the immediate focus of IAOBM was on athletes, membership has grown to include other professionals. Accountants, financial planners, and attorneys make up more of the members than the athletes and entertainers, but Darrin says, "We are here to work together and help each other, regardless of the vocation."

The total number of members is 125, up from 30 in March of 1998. "Our present goal is educational, not to get a million members," Darrin emphasizes. "We want to help the members know how to build better businesses, how to get loans, how to write business plans, etc." When this is accomplished, men of color across the nation will be making a larger impact in their businesses and communities, and that is what excites Darrin.

Though IAOBM is making waves in influential circles, Darrin is not a man who has had life handed to him on a silver platter. In fact, it was just the opposite.

Rough Practice

Darrin grew up in Miami, the youngest in a family of five. For him, life was normal: his father worked and his mother stayed home to take care of the children. Then, without warning, everything changed.

One weekend, when Darrin was only three, his dad was helping organize a neighborhood carnival to raise money for a police benevolence fund. The streets were barricaded off, but one belligerent driver refused to follow directions. As Mr. Smith told the driver to go around, the car reversed, backing over Mr. Smith's foot. In the process, the driver got out and complained that Mr. Smith had chipped the paint on the side of the car.

In a mad rage, the driver sped off, only to return a short time later with a loaded pistol. When he saw Mr. Smith, he chased him down and shot him in the back. Young Darrin's four siblings, all between the ages of 9 and 12, were present at the time of the shooting. Mr. Smith died at the hospital the same day.

Suddenly, everything was turned upside down. The children lost their stay-at-home mom, as she was forced to find a full time job, and the family moved across town.

Mrs. Smith was no quitter. She worked hard and kept the family together, which always included attending church on Sunday mornings. "Mom was a God-fearing woman," Darrin states. "She taught us the little things, like how to be humble and that God will bless you when you bless others." Though at times she would be overly generous and give too much away, he recalls, "she was always investing in us." Today, Darrin's two older sisters are teachers, recently graduating from college with honors, one brother works for a printing company, and the other is a fireman. "All the credit goes to God and to my mother," Darrin says fondly, "She's the greatest person in the world."

But even in the hard times, Darrin remembers, "God was bringing people into my life for a reason." After his dad died, Darrin was paired with Seymore Marksman as part of the Big Brothers & Big Sisters program. For almost 20 years Marksman has been a friend and confidant, and Darrin adds, "He was always putting a book in my face."

Life's Coaches

When Darrin was 7, he started playing organized football. Even on the field, Darrin was finding individuals to mentor him. In fact, it was the football coaches who were some of the most influential men in his life. "They were father-figures for me," he says, and through these relationships, not to mention playing good ball, Darrin ended up at the University of Miami on a football scholarship.

Under coach Jimmy Johnson, Darrin's team won two championships, and then when Darrin graduated, he was drafted in the second round by Dallas Cowboys in 1993. The Cowboys, under coach Jimmy Johnson, won the Super Bowl his rookie year and then again two years later.

While in Dallas, he went to a Wednesday night Bible study at Oak Cliff Bible Fellowship. Darrin's mother had met the church's pastor, Pastor Tony Evans, a few weeks earlier in Florida and had told him, "Take care of my baby." When Pastor Tony introduced himself to Darrin, who is 6'2" and weighs 240 pounds, he said, "You are no baby." After explaining himself, and the chance meeting with Darrin's mother, he invited Darrin to start meeting regularly with him. Pastor Tony encouraged him and challenged him in his walk with God, and as Darrin points out, "He has been a coach, a mentor and a big influence in my life." Another coach and mentor has been Pastor

E. K. Bailey of Concord Baptist Church, with whom Darrin struck up a close friendship while in Dallas. Even now, while playing in Seattle, the mentoring relationships continue. "They stay on me regardless of where I am," Darrin says with a smile.

Leonardo Starke, an attorney and a member of IAOBM since its inception, has known Darrin for eight years and says, "Darrin has done a good job standing up to the pressures associated with being a pro-athlete and being in the media's spotlight." The fact that Darrin is "humble, driven, caring, goal-oriented, and studious," as Starke describes him, has helped shape the lives of other athletes and individuals who become associated with Darrin.

Coaching and mentoring is really what IAOBM is all about. "I believe we are here for two reasons," Darrin notes. "First, to serve God, and second, to serve others." By teaching others how important it is to give, plan and invest, the spiritual foundation of the organization shines through. The potential for positively impacting the next generation grows exponentially as education and practical understanding increase.

It's a shame that Joe Louis wasn't able to meet Darrin Smith. It would have changed history, again.

Money!
Measuring Wealth

by Guy Carlson

How much is enough? Is money bad? What constitutes success? Is prosperity for everyone? Can you take it with you?

Bill Gates, the world's richest man, saw his net worth jump 40 percent for the fourth straight year to equal almost 90 billion as of May, 1999. Incredibly, Bill Gates has a value greater than the gross domestic product of many countries. It is impossible to give an exact worth for people like Gates whose wealth is tied up largely in the stock market where unprecedented milestones are being reached almost daily.

In 1996 there were nearly 450 billionaires in the world, 149 of which were American citizens. In 1986, when there were about 150 billionaires, 0.5 percent of all households in the U.S. had assets worth $1 million or more. Today, that percentage has increased to 3.5 percent, which is equivalent to 3,500,000 millionaires in the U.S. alone. Most of this wealth is not old money, and not even inflation can keep pace with what we are seeing in today's market. Even the most optimistic forecast five years ago did not project the euphoric conditions of today's market.

The newfound wealth of so many Americans comes in the midst of a rising gulf between the rich and poor. Society mirrors corporate downsizing of the 1990s with the thinning of the middle class: there are a few at the top, a lot at the bottom, and middle management has felt the squeeze. Unemployment figures are down, but under the surface the disenfranchised professionals and middle managers have filled the ranks of the burgeoning consulting sector of the economy.

America, with a rising number of self-employed and home businesses, is still the land of opportunity. Many of the over six billion people who live around the globe will work 10 years or more to make what an average American worker does in just one year. It is virtually impossible to travel to any country without being met with abject poverty.

Money is not bad

What observation can be made from all of this? Among Christians, the subject of money is especially controversial. Ask any 10 people their opinion and you will likely receive as many different answers. Many Christians choose to categorize the issues of money and wealth as unspiritual, while overlooking the significance it has in our lives. Author, Howard Dayton, says one out of every 10 verses in the Bible concerns money, possessions, lending, savings or other related issues. The Bible has more to say about money than any other issue!

In 1991, authors James Patterson and Peter Kim collected an unbiased random sampling of 3,577 people across the country. Their book, *The Day America Told the Truth*, explains what respondents would be willing to do for $10 million. Among the results were:

- 25% would abandon their family
- 23% would turn to prostitution
- 10% would let a murderer go free
- 7% would commit murder

The responses showed little variation when the coveted amount was dropped to $3 million.

But money is not evil. The things people will do for money is. Money is simply an inanimate object of exchange. It has no capacity for good or evil. As with all things, our heart attitude is of utmost importance to God.

Those who chase after riches fall into temptation and a snare and many foolish and harmful desires which plunge men into ruin and destruction. For the love of money is a root of all sorts of evil (1 Timothy 6:9-10).

What matters is our attitude toward wealth and what we do with it.

God wants us to prosper

Abraham, David, Solomon and Joseph were all very wealthy. It was the pleasure of God to bless them in this manner. Solomon was given the chance by God to ask for anything he wanted, and he chose wisdom. As a reward for his heart attitude, he not only received wisdom, but also became the richest man on earth.

Many Christians labor under the misconception that riches and holiness are incompatible. Piety and poverty are not necessarily good bedfellows. In fact, one indicator of righteous living is prosperity. Just as an earthly father delights in giving gifts to his children, so does our heavenly Father. The Bible is abundant with promises of gifts from God, including prosperity:

...let the Lord be magnified, who has pleasure in the prosperity of his servant (Psalm 35:27).

...meditate on My Word day and night; for then will your way be prosperous and you will have great success. (Joshua 1:7-8).

A faithful man will abound with blessings... (Proverbs 28:19).

By humility and the fear of the Lord come riches, honor and life (Luke 6:38).

Does wealth = success?

That depends on how you define success! Wealth that really counts is stored in heaven. Our lifetime is but a moment on the scale of eternity. What we accumulate here stays here. Not everyone is destined to be wealthy. God has placed men and women at all levels of affluence to touch the lives of others. At the very least, however, God promises that all of our needs will be met. Beyond that, it is up to His pleasure and our faithfulness.

Success for the whole man encompasses the total of his being. Are you healthy? Do you have a good relationship with your wife? Are your children a blessing? Are you fulfilling your God-given destiny? Are you helping others to achieve their destiny? What have you done with what you have been given? Are you pleasing God in everything you do?

Our name may never appear on the list of Forbes 500, but it is another list that is most important. When the race is finished and you stand before the judge, the successful scorecard will read something like this: "Your name has been written in the Book of Life. Well done good and faithful servant. Enter now into your reward."

Money as a goal

Money is one of the fruits of faithful living, but we should not put our hope in money, or make it our goal. Wherever your treasure is, there your heart will also be.

In his book, *Answers To Your Family's Financial Questions*, author Larry Burkett says, "God clearly desires that we prosper and that we enjoy the fruits of our labor. However, in the United States I believe that we've stretched this principle beyond the boundaries of common sense. We need bigger and better indulgences to keep us content."

The answer to the challenge of keeping money in proper perspective is quite simple. All the wealth of the world belongs to the Creator of the universe, not to mention the fact that our very bodies are His as well. We are simply stewards of the talents and resources He has entrusted to us for as long as we live. It is not the accumulation of things, but the stewardship of what we have that matters. The question of how much you own is really a misnomer, since you really don't own anything.

For most of us this will require a shift in our paradigm. This will dramatically affect our ability to give in ways that do not directly benefit us. A refreshing freedom comes when we are not tied to our money. The tendency to hoard is replaced with liberality. With liberality comes joy—the joy of giving—and the pleasure of seeing the needs and dreams of others being met. Giving has become the reward

Why do the unrighteous prosper?

If one sign of faithfulness is financial blessing, then why is there so much wealth in the hands of people who do not live by godly principles? I can attribute this to one or more of the following:

#1. Many Christians have abdicated the position of being good stewards over the vast richness of God's creation. Though this is a sad commentary on the state of the Christian community, it is nonetheless true.

#2. Wealth is only one indicator of spiritual blessing. Blessings are not always in monetary form. After salvation, I count my wife and children as my richest treasures. Peace, contentment, the love of committed friends, a pleasant countenance, good health, and the fulfillment that comes through accomplishing my God-given destiny are a few of the others. Wealth in the absence of these is less the result of righteous living and more a testament to the human tenacity in the pursuit of riches.

How many celebrity marriages end up in divorce? How many affluent people turn to suicide, drugs and alcohol to ease the pain of discouragement? How many executives reach the top of the corporate ladder leaving a legacy of pain in their wake? How many children and wives end up in a pile of broken dreams as the price for those who make it to the top? The blessing of the Lord comes without sorrow! The blessing of the Lord makes rich, and he adds no sorrow to it (Proverbs 10:22).

#3. Financial prosperity sometimes comes to those who don't deserve it. After all, the rain falls on the just and the unjust alike.

We can't take it with us

Matthew 19:24 says, "It is more difficult for a rich man to enter the kingdom of heaven than for a camel to pass through the eye of a needle." This illustration was given to demonstrate how easy it is to become attached to riches. Wealth can be a sign of God's blessing on our lives. It is the pursuit of riches that leads to compromise.

The safest way to avoid greed is to become a giver, so give generously. I have identified three reasons God grants wealth to individuals:

1.   As a testimony of faithful living
2.   As a blessing or reward
3.   To bless others

The last of these is the most important. It is impossible to out-give the blessings of God. The more you give, the more you can be trusted with. In this way you are God's instrument to invest in the lives of others, and you become a valuable resource to fund the work of the Kingdom of God.

Guy Carlson is the Publisher of The Christian Businessman magazine, the premier magazine for complete success— personally, spiritually, and financially.

Faithful On All Accounts

Larry Burkett

Faithful On All Accounts

Larry Burkett, founder and president of Christian Financial Concepts, never imagined his words would be worth their weight in gold.

by Rob Dilbone

Like most responsible, young husbands and fathers in the early '60s, Larry Burkett was consumed with his work and getting an education. He believed there was a God but says he "just didn't care enough to have a relationship with Him." My how things change. In 1970 Larry walked down the aisle of the Park Avenue Church in Titusville, Florida, and accepted Jesus Christ as his Lord and Savior and his life took on a whole new direction. Today, Christian Financial Concepts (CFC), the non-profit ministry of which he is Founder and President, reaches tens of thousands of people each day with Bible-based financial advice. His radio program is heard on over 1,300 stations daily and several of his books have been best sellers. CFC is changing lives by educating people on what God's Word has to say about their finances. Today, Larry Burkett is truly a testimony to how God can use a willing vessel to teach His people.

Beginnings

In 1939 as America was finally emerging from the grip of the Great Depression, Lawrence Allen Burkett was born. He was the middle child of nine children in what he describes as a "dysfunctional, non-Christian home." Although the Burkett household was not totally devoid of love, his mother was simply tired of children and the struggles of life. "By the time I came along," recalls Larry, "it was pretty much everyone for themselves. I don't remember ever feeling loved at all." At the time of his birth his father had not held a full-time job in six years.

The Depression made a lasting impact on his parents and they never really recovered from its ill effects. Like many who lived through it, they lived in constant fear that one day another depression would come and take away everything. It was that fear that kept the family in a lifestyle of poverty. "Looking back I don't think we were actually as poor as we lived," Larry says. "If we had some extra money we didn't dare spend it for fear that there might be another depression next year. My parents were fearful to take the next step and I hated that. I determined that I was going to make money and never be poor again."

Larry's parents had a simple rule: anything the boys wanted other than food, they had to earn themselves. Consequently, Larry started working weekends when he was nine and says he "doesn't remember not working." From nine until he was 14 he earned a living as a singer. In those days the movie theaters had live entertainment between shows, so during the double and triple features on a Saturday he was part of the act. One of the girls he sang with, named Julie Byrd, ran off to New York at age 16 and became an actress on Broadway.

Larry, however, had decided early on that he wanted a family. He met Judy Morgan in high school and they were married before she graduated. Their early years were hectic ones with Larry entering the Air Force and then going on to college. Larry says he started going to college because "I knew that in my generation a college education was the only way to get ahead." He realized he needed a job to pay for his education, so he went to work at Cape Canaveral. For the next seven years he got up at 3 a.m. and went to work until 3 p.m., then drove an hour and a half to school, went to class for four hours and then drove an hour and a half back home. "Of course Judy and I had no relationship as you can well imagine," says Larry. "I was gone 100% of the time and she was left to rear our four children alone. I only knew my children in passing."

Salvation

About the time Larry was finishing his education, Judy got saved. She went to a little Southern Baptist church and almost immediately there were concerned Christians coming around the Burkett home sharing Christ with her wayward husband. Larry felt that his wife's newly found faith might help her cope with life, but he had neither time nor any interest in going to church. "I ran a department for GE at the space center where we basically did most of the experiments on the early unmanned and later on the manned Mercury, Gemini and Apollo rockets. I encountered a lot of people who were true atheists. I wasn't an atheist," Larry recalls, "but I was an agnostic. I thought there was a God, but I didn't really care one way or the other."

For the next three years Judy's friends from church came around and tried to witness to Larry. He listened patiently for a time and then began to tire of all the unwanted attention and began to argue with his well-intentioned guests. The pastor, Peter Lord, had been visiting as well and it was on his sixth visit that things came to a head. "I was sick and tired of it," Larry recalls, "so I would argue every point he made. Finally, he got so angry he got up and stormed out of the house, slamming the door as he left. Then about 20 seconds later he stuck his head back in and said, 'You know what Burkett, you're going to hell!' Then he slammed the door again and left."

The next time Larry saw Pastor Lord was when he walked down the aisle at his church and accepted Christ. "We have been good friends ever since," says Larry. "He was the greatest influence in my early Christian walk. He really made a lasting impact on my life."

Ministry

Larry began to grow quickly in his Christian walk and before long Pastor Lord asked him to teach the church's new members class. "That is the best thing he could have ever done for me," says Larry. "He forced me to learn quickly." Teaching that class really laid the foundation of his life-long walk with God.

By the time he accepted Christ, Larry had left the space center and become the vice president of an electronics company. The company was growing and prospects looked very good when Larry came to the conclusion that God had something else for him to do. He began to look around for what he might do. "I was about a two-year-old Christian when I first met Dr. Bill Bright of Campus Crusade (CCC) for Christ at what they called The Lay Institute for Evangelism. He had been talking with a mutual friend about starting a financial ministry of some type to help resolve some of the problems they were having with new staff members." It seems that a lot of the Campus Crusade recruits would come out of college with more zeal to go on staff than finances to support themselves. Many ended up in credit card debt unable to fulfill their commitment to the ministry.

Larry's friend told Dr. Bright that he knew someone with a great financial background looking for something to do. "The next thing I knew Bill came to me and said, 'You ought to be on Campus Crusade's staff,'" says Larry. About six months later Larry left the electronics company and joined the CCC staff. He spent the next couple of years counseling the staff on financial matters and traveling around the country helping set up budgets for future staff members. He also began teaching Biblical principles of handling money to groups of Christian Businessmen at his local church. "Everyone had to take a turn at teaching," recalls Larry, "and finances is what interested me out of the Bible. So right in line with that old cliche, 'In the land of the blind a one-eyed man can become King,' I kind of became our resident counselor on what the Bible says about finances."

People began to ask Larry to teach on biblical finances to their Bible studies and eventually he began to do so on a larger scale. After two and a half years at Campus Crusade he was doing about 40 conferences a year and began to wonder if teaching on the biblical principles of finances might be what God had called him to do. He left the staff of Campus Crusade, called an attorney friend in Atlanta and incorporated what is now Christian Financial Concepts." The Lord blessed that decision and continues to do so.

A Helping Hand

Larry soon realized that teaching was something he always wanted to do but thought it would not pay enough to accomplish his goal of being financially free. Teaching was a logical step in the progression of things God had already equipped him to do. As the ministry grew another logical step was getting into radio, which he did in 1982 when Dr. James Dobson called and asked if Larry would come by and do an interview for his program.

They ended up doing a dozen programs and Larry began to get calls from station managers asking if he had anything else they could air on their stations. "Then I got a call from a station manager in Chattanooga offering to rent a studio in Atlanta if I would go and record some basic material to air on his station. So that's how I got into radio. I had no intention of doing all this; God just opened the doors. The Lord knew there was a need and that His people needed to hear this message, so He just provided a vehicle to do it."

Cancer

Most of Larry's fight with cancer is depicted in his book *Damaged but Not Broken* (Moody Press, 1996). Since the book came out he has learned some things about himself. "I guess the thing that does not come through in the book," he says, "is that this has been a growing process for me. It's been a confirmation that God never gives more than you need before you need it, only when you need it. God has given me what He promised: peace. I'm not naive about it. I understand I could die from cancer, but I also know nothing can take me from this early until God is ready for me to go."

Larry doesn't have an unrealistic attitude about who he is either. "I don't expect any rewards nor do I deserve any. I tell God with all my heart, 'Hey, if You will just let me into Heaven that's enough. Heaven will be enough of a reward for me.'"

Priorities

Larry is very quick to proclaim his number one priority—"to know Christ better." He does regret not spending more time with his children back when he was a workaholic before he got saved. Shortly after he accepted Christ he was awakened in the night with a Scripture verse planted in his mind. He got up and searched through his Bible until he found Psalm 127:2 "What vanity it is that you arise early in the morning, staying late in the evening in pursuit of riches—for God shall give to those He loves even when they sleep." In keeping with a promise he made to God to never be disobedient to His Word, Larry made a commitment to never work over 50 hours a week again. And he never has and says he "never will." But that commitment cannot bring back time lost, so he is now sowing as much time as he possibly can into his grandchildren.

"I think it is very difficult, if not impossible, to be a successful Christian businessman and not have your family behind you," Larry says. "You cannot be totally defeated in one area and a success in another. You have to have your family. I have never heard a wealthy man on his deathbed saying, 'I wish I had spent more time making money.' Instead, he says, "I wish I had spent more time with my wife, my kids, and my grandkids."

Larry feels an urgency to educate parents and young people about finances in order to reach the next generation before they get corrupted. "Helping the current generation is important," he says, "but in large part they are very difficult to reach so we have to hunt and peck and find those who want to change." Larry believes that CCC's message is urgent for the younger generations. He adds, "Parents need to teach their children how to be proper stewards, because if they don't someone else is out there teaching them the wrong values."

Ultimately it is up to the elder generation to equip the younger to handle the challenges they will face in their Christian walk. Whether we will rally together to make the changes necessary to protect the next generation is hard to say. But with leaders like Larry Burkett carrying God's message to His people, there is still hope.

Rob Dilbone was former Editor for The Christian Businessman magazine. He resides in Gainesville, Florida, with his wife and daughter.

Truth In Selling

By Michael Pink

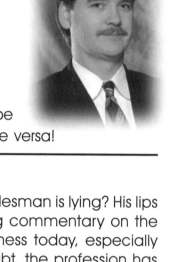

When truth and selling are in the same sentence, the results may be better than you imagined—or vice versa!

"How do you know when a salesman is lying? His lips are moving!" That joke is a biting commentary on the state of affairs in American business today, especially the sales profession. Without doubt, the profession has earned its reputation, but it need not be true of everyone in the field of sales. In fact, I am convinced that an honest man has an advantage in an environment permeated with liars. Liars are eventually found out and have a difficult time regaining trust, and trust is the highest form of human motivation, at least when it comes to business. The only way a liar can survive long-term in the business arena is to move from one city to the next or change industries every few of years.

I remember one forty-something-year-old sales veteran who told me frankly, "The fact that I don't always tell the truth is your problem—not mine!" He not only believed that nobody was getting hurt when he lied but that lying was in fact necessary in some cases to get the business. He didn't believe that a Biblically based, integrity-oriented sales approach could work in the real world. He was wrong!

His company had retained me to do a sales and marketing analysis and part of that analysis was spending a few days with him in the field. On one call, after misrepresenting some facts to the prospect and not taking the time to discover their real needs, he proceeded to use traditional strong arm tactics to "close" the sale. He tried the "special price if you buy today" close, the "alternative choice" close and even the old "Ben Franklin" close, all without success. Finally, having decided that this was not for him, the business owner with whom we were meeting politely asked us to leave.

The sad part was that the service being offered was ideal for this business owner, but the salesman had broken the golden rule in trust building. Because he lied, coerced and manipulated, he lost the sale! I was in pain watching this ordeal unfold in front of me and finally felt compelled to speak up, though I was not well versed on the service being offered. I spoke truthfully, asked some piercing questions, empathized with the owner, restated the offer in precise and accurate terms, then gave him the opportunity to accept the offer, which if implemented, would significantly impact his business in a positive manner. What he heard made sense to him and it was spoken with compassion and in truth. Truth is always more powerful than a lie, and genuine compassion goes a long way towards forging any agreement. This time, he bought!

The sales rep was shocked! He had already packed up his briefcase and was standing up to leave before I spoke my first words. He witnessed the power of the truth, being spoken without apology, yet in a kind and compelling manner. When we left the customer's office, the sales rep had just earned $1,000 commission and was now much more receptive to my biblically based sales approach. He tried to adapt those ways and for the next two or three months he actually tripled his sales, but his old nature got the better of him and he eventually forgot what really worked best and fell back to his old ways. Sounds like the pattern of ancient Israel to me. Changing your ways without changing your heart will never last!

How to really increase sales

Dishonesty in sales is not limited to a few home siding salesman as depicted by actor Danny Devito in *Tin Man* or used car salesmen as shown by Robin Williams in *Cadillac Man*. In fact, a few years ago, the 75th anniversary issue of Sales & Marketing Management magazine devoted its cover story to the near fatal free fall of IBM stock that lost 70 percent of its value and forced the company to eliminate about 40,000 sales-related positions. According to former salesman Bill Gardner, "We were so well trained, we could sell anything, good or bad. So under quota pressures, we sold systems that our customers didn't need, didn't want and couldn't afford." This lapse in integrity gave a whole new meaning to blue chip stocks.

Twelve years ago, when I first moved to the United States, I took a job selling copiers. It's a highly competitive, often cut-throat business that churns through sales reps like frogs in a blender! You have to stay on top to survive and no one survives without scars. On my first day there, the vice president of sales laid out the ground rules. He expected no sales my first month, two the second month and four-per-month thereafter. I was to sell one copier out of every four or five I demonstrated. The national average was one out of four.

When I came home from work that day, my wife asked what was troubling me. I told her that they expected me to sell one copier for every four I demonstrated. She asked, "What was wrong with that?" I told her that it meant I had to accept a 75% failure rate and I wasn't about to accept those kind of numbers. Instead, I was going to study the Scriptures and find principles and strategies that I could apply to sales and instead of settling for one out of four—I was intending to sell one out of one!

Not only did she think I was a little crazy, but the branch manager to whom I reported the next day was positive he had made a poor hiring decision when he heard my "unrealistic" goals. Nevertheless, I set out on my mission, Bible in hand. The first passage God opened up to me was Proverbs 3:3-4, "Let not mercy and truth forsake you; Bind them around your neck, Write them on the tablet of your heart, And so find favor and high esteem in the sight of God and man." Well obviously, to obtain the goal I had in mind, I would need all the "favor" I could find.

For me, binding truth around my neck meant not only telling the truth but also practicing full disclosure. You can tell the truth but convey a lie. For example: I spoke at a Promise Keepers rally with nearly 60,000 men in attendance. That's the truth. But only the guys in my row could hear me because I was seated in the nose-bleed section! That's full disclosure. You can make truthful statements yet paint a very inaccurate picture. Many sales people consider themselves honest because they didn't actually lie, yet they allowed a customer to believe something they knew was a lie. To me, that's still lying.

I also take telling the truth one step further. Make sure you not only tell the truth and practice full disclosure of relevant facts, but take the responsibility to ensure that

98

your prospect understands what you've told them. I've had customers understand something quite different than I was trying to convey and it caused problems that had to be resolved.

After 90 days in the field selling copiers, I was attending the quarterly sales meeting and reported that I had done only 22 demonstrations. I was supposed to have also made 5 sales during that time period, which I had never seen a new rep accomplish in the two years I was with that company. I then went on to report that I had also made 22 sales, three and a half times a goal that had never been hit and a sale to demonstration ratio of one out of one! Unheard of and totally unrealistic, unless of course you believe in the power of God's Word and are willing to submit yourself to its rule.

Now I make my living sharing with others Biblical principles and strategies that can be successfully applied to the selling process. The good news is that what I've learned is transferable and others are reaping wonderful results as they too submit themselves to the authority of God's Word and apply it to their careers. Try it, you'll like the results!

Michael Q. Pink, best selling author, speaker and creator of the "Selling Among Wolves—Without Joining The Pack!" Sales coaching program, is founder of the Strategic Resource Institute, providing Biblical solutions for maximizing the impact of sales and marketing strategies. Contact him at: SRI, 5642 N. Via-Umbrosa, Tuscan, AZ 85750. Tel: (520)-615-0870 or visit his website at www.sellingamongwolves.com.

Going Out in Style

Paul J Meyer

GOING OUT IN STYLE

With most men amassing wealth, why is highly successful entrepreneur Paul J. Meyer making plans to die broke?

by Brian Mast

To die broke implies that you had something to give away. Self-made millionaire Paul J. Meyer definitely has something to give away. He formed his first business at age 21 and continues his entrepreneurial interests even today as he begins his eighth decade of life. Among other business interests, Meyer Family Enterprises encompasses personal achievement courses, leadership training, educational computer software, a personal achievement television network, aircraft sales, an auto racing facility, manufacturing trucks, autos, and bus parts, residential and commercial real estate development, fiberglass products, printing, exotic game ranching, and international trade. For each business under his mantle of leadership, he has pursued two goals: to operate at a profit and to be debt free. With more than 40 businesses owned and operated today by the Meyer family, he is doing quite well. All the Meyer businesses are profitable, and 75 percent are debt free.

In 1997, at the age of 70, Meyer formally retired from actively serving as the CEO of the Meyer family businesses. His retirement gives him more time to pursue personal interests. However, Meyer has not tried very hard to appear retired, and some even doubt that he ever intended to slow down in the first place. He is still working, but focuses his time on fulfilling his life mission or calling.

Meyer says with passion, "My objective is to continue developing and using the skills, talents, and gifts God has given me to make the world a better place." One of Meyer's favorite affirmations is from John Wesley: to do all the good I can with all the people I can in all the places I can as long as I can. To accomplish this objective, Meyer plans on using whatever additional years are allotted to him to continue to build the Paul J. Meyer Family Foundation. Over the past two to three decades, a large percentage of the Meyer income has gone directly into charities and missions. He accurately paraphrases the Bible when he says, "Your heart is where your pocket book is." He has taken this truth to heart.

In fact, when it comes down to it, Meyer explains, "We intend to sell our properties and companies and place that money in our foundation to perpetuate the charities and interests we have." The Meyers have already started this process. Many of the family owned companies are managed by a trustee group, some have been gifted and turned over to appointed individuals, and others are in trusts for the Meyer children.

Retired (Mostly)

In Waco, Texas, where his home and offices are located, Meyer now goes to his office whenever he desires. "I try to make every hour of my life count for Christ. I also try to multiply the effectiveness of that hour a hundred times." For example, he has helped several charities set up development departments and to establish foundations. As Meyer puts it, "I like to put overalls on money and put it to work so that it multiplies over and over."

When in Texas, Meyer and his wife Jane spend at least one day each week at Summers Mill Retreat and

Conference Center. They gave the entire farm to charity several years ago for use as a Christian retreat and conference center.

Meyer also pays close attention to his health. Wherever he is, he exercises daily for an hour and a half. When he is at their home near Aspen, Colorado, he and Jane walk several hours each day. In addition, they participate in golf, tennis, and mountain biking.

A considerable amount of his time and money is spent working with the poor. One of his favorite organizations, Mission Waco, has as a major thrust the Church Under the Bridge. On Sundays, poor people gather together under a busy overpass and are fed by local churches. Chairs are set up and volunteers feed those with a multiplicity of problems—drug addicts, those in halfway houses, recovering alcoholics, and others living on the streets. Meyer asks, "Where would Christ be today if He were in town? Who would He help? Who would He talk to? I believe those are the places we need to be, all the time, not just around Christmas time."

The Meyers have also invested much of their income and time into the Haggai Institute for Advanced Leadership. The Haggai Institute specializes in evangelism and leadership training of individuals from Third World countries. These individuals then return to their own countries to train others. Meyer says with amazement, "Some of the graduates of Haggai Institute have already trained over 3,000 people in their own countries!" With two-thirds of the developing nations closed to western missionaries, Meyer believes this is one of the best routes to reach the world's population with the gospel of Christ.

Tightwads Among Us

Though Meyer gives a lot of his money away, such is not the case among most wealthy individuals. "But they have their reasons why they can't give," as Meyer explains. "They say they can't give because they have debts. They give excuses because they trust themselves and not God." In addition, he points out, "Those who can give a lot give a mere one and a half percent of their income." The wealth is already there, Meyer notes, "enough to change the social fabric of every community."

The potential for changing his community in Waco, Texas, excites Meyer. He explains that God has placed enough people with the wealth to take care of all the needs in every community without the help of the federal government. Though the potential is promising, Meyer has observed the darker side of some wealthy individuals. "When people make their top priority the acquisition of material possessions," Meyer explains, "they progressively become more selfish, self-centered, egotistical, and proud. When J. Paul Getty was asked how much was enough, he held up his hand and said, 'Just a little bit more.'"

To make matters worse, many churchgoers give far less to their churches and communities than they could. Meyer notes with disappointment, "I came across statistics indicating the majority of those who regularly attend church (30-40 times per year) never give a cent!"

Meyer has more than enough to say to those who aren't making an impact in the communities, but he prefers to let his actions speak for themselves. After all, he says, "I have always believed that what you do is more important and than what you say.

106

Several years ago, he and Jane put $5 million dollars into a foundation they named Passport to Success. Through this foundation they would guarantee financial assistance for many of the economically disadvantaged people in the Waco area. With the help of the Meyers and several other Waco families, more than 500 youth are currently receiving financial assistance to attend college. The majority of students who participate in this program are minorities and from one-parent homes. "Helping these individuals is a dream I have had for a long, long time," Meyer notes with joy.

He envisions the day, as he says, "when business people in every town in America are doing the same thing." The results of such a venture would be citizens who can stand on their own feet, pay their taxes, get off welfare, and become productive citizens and good role models in their community.

Having started Passport to Success over 10 years ago, Meyer has seen his efforts come to fruition. A few years ago the first PTS student graduated from Baylor University. At a special reception, the young man, who had recently started his own business in Dallas, Texas, was asked to say a few words. When he finished speaking, he took out his checkbook and wrote a check for $1,000 to the Passport to Success Foundation.

Hard Work and Dreams

Growing up in California during the Great Depression did influence Meyer, but it was his parents who made a lasting impression on his attitude toward life and work. At the age of five, he was picking fruit with other migrant farm workers. When the foreman complained that Paul was too young to be working, Paul's father said, "Well, we want him to learn to work."

Young Meyer got it from both ends. One extremely hot day, while working in a grape vineyard and returning home with a bloody nose, he asked his mother, "How long do I have to do this kind of work?" She replied, "Until you develop the gifts that God gave you." She cradled his head and said, "This is a magic carpet. When you develop it, it will take you anywhere you want to go, and you can be anything you want to be."

From that moment on, Meyer says, "I made up my mind that people and words were going to be my pursuits." The next day, while working in the fields, Meyer made a pivotal decision. "I prayed and asked Jesus Christ to come into my life. I wanted to follow Him and develop the talents and abilities He gave to me, and that has been my lifelong pursuit."

At the age of 19, after military service, he began selling life insurance. By the age of 27 he had acquired his first million. He then spent two years as Sales Executive for Word, Inc., increasing sales by 1500 percent. By 1960, he founded Success Motivation Institute, Inc. and shortly thereafter Leadership Management, Inc. These firms were established for the purpose of helping people develop their personal potential and their leadership skills

Over the years, the product line has expanded to include more than 20 full-length programs designed to help people use more of their potential for greater success. These materials have been translated into 21 languages for more than 60 countries with combined sales exceeding $1.5 billion worldwide, establishing Meyer as the pre-eminent leader in the self-improvement industry.

Like he determined as a young boy, Meyer has successfully made people and words his pursuit. But he isn't finished yet. He has more words to write, more people to impact, and a whole lot more giving yet to do.

SELLING AMONG WOLVES
Without Joining the Pack

by Michael Pink

Why Nice Guys Finish First

Recently a Colorado businessman told me that his business was hurting because he refused to lower his standards and use high pressure, manipulative sales techniques to close business. His competition on the other hand apparently had no scruples and seemed to be prospering despite their use of heavy handed, high pressure "closing" techniques and other questionable selling tactics. He was beginning to believe the lie that "Nice guys finish last!" He felt he would have to choose between his convictions or profits, as if they were somehow mutually exclusive.

I think nice guys can finish first, but I also think nice guys are men who compete vigorously, though fairly. Being nice does not imply being a doormat. Doormats do finish last! In sales, a nice guy will find ways to outserve his competition, not provide mediocre service and complain about the ravenous competition when he loses the sale. Nice guys excel in providing the best service, the best product and the most innovative ideas in the most clear, concise and compelling manner. To quote one writer, they don't "flinch in the face of sacrifice, hesitate in the presence of the adversary, negotiate at the table of the enemy, ponder at the pool of popularity, or meander in the maze of mediocrity." Indeed, they function with excellence in the marketplace and are a witness to the nations!

The Colorado businessman mentioned above needed to learn biblical principles and strategies adapted to the selling process and incorporate them into his business. His average sale was just under $1,000, typically a one call close. Because not every prospect was ready to purchase on the first meeting and he being a "nice guy," he often walked away empty handed, and his competition would swoop in, not leaving without a signed contract or a police escort!

If I were selling home security systems and my mother was a good candidate for one but wanted some time to think it over, I wouldn't lose the sale to a competitor during the interim no matter how slick, polished or pressuring he was. Why? Because of the rapport and the trust I have established with my mother. In fact, even if my product were more expensive than the competition's I would still get the sale. So how can we get these principles of trust and rapport working for us with total strangers?

This often overlooked approach to building trust in sales is more important than skill, technique or motivation, though all are important. A Florida man once called me stating that he was starting his first job in sales in just a few days. He was scared, unskilled and unprepared to provide for his family on a straight commission job with no guarantees or cash advances. He was desperate for help and asked me to train him over the phone on how to sell.

I explained that the skills he needed would take years to develop and he didn't have that much time. He needed to grasp the foundational principles of selling and function out of an understanding of those principles. Although the necessary skills would come in time, it was possible to begin applying those principles for an immediate impact. He believed me and took copious notes. A week later he called me with the results. He had made eight presentations and secured eight sales for a first week commission check of $3,000! Needless to say, this man became an ardent believer in a "principle based" approach to sales and continued on in a highly successful career.

Going back to our man in Colorado, he needed to recognize that 90% of the decision to buy is made in the heart and the other 10% is simply the mind needing to justify what the heart wants. In short, he had to learn how to win the battle for the heart. If he could win that battle, no high pressure competitor would take the sale away anymore than a high pressure suitor would have convinced my fiancée (now my wife) to marry him instead of me.

Winning the Heart

So how do we win the battle for the heart? The overriding principle here is to "serve with all your heart, from the heart, to win the heart." It's been said that Canaan, as referenced in the Bible, is a representation of the heart or soul and that Joshua is a representation of the born again spirit man. Joshua was to subdue and conquer the land of Canaan, bringing the land into subjection to the government of God, much like our spirit man in submission to God's Spirit brings our soul into subjection to the government (kingdom) of God.

So what do you do with the domineering, terror invoking individuals are hostile and use intimidation to get what they want? In sales, these type of people demand price concessions, unreasonable delivery schedules, etc. They operate on a win/lose basis: they win—you lose. When you encounter such individuals (someone who is openly hostile, intimidating and demanding their own way), you must diffuse their hostility and intimidation before you can develop a fiercely loyal customer.

At the root of their terrorizing antics is their own terror—their fear of failure, their fear of rejection, and their fear of being hurt or being taken advantage of. You may have heard it said that "hurting people hurt others, while healed people heal others." I would like to submit that terrorized people terrorize others and that confident people, well, they look terror in the face and give them the security they're really looking for.

I remember a Canadian businessman I was trying to sell a copier to in 1978. When I walked in the lobby of his office, he walked past and said to the secretary in a rude and gruff voice, "Get rid of him!" I politely declined his offer and walked over to where he was standing in the center of the office. I believe my boldness surprised him—it did me! When he looked me in the face, I was polite, kind, courteous and confident. He directed me to a manager who later made the purchase from me. My strategy was simple: minister in the opposite spirit.

He was operating out of fear, but I was operating out of boldness that comes from the Lord. He was rude and intimidating, while I was polite and engaging. My confidence earned his respect if not his envy. My kindness in the face of his rudeness captured a part of his heart and for a moment, he allowed me entrance into his business and life. From there I simply outserved my competitors and easily won the business.

Some say a nice guy would have left after the boss demanded his removal from the office. But I was too nice to let him purchase what I believed to be an inferior product for a higher price. I was too nice to let myself become another notch on his belt of salesmen he had kicked out of his office and would one day have to answer for. I was too nice to let him get away with being a total jerk that day. Instead, I confronted him with kindness and the love of Christ exhibited with confidence, and it carried the day.

Too often we try to be nicer than Jesus and when we get beaten in the marketplace, we blame it on the bad guys. We hide behind our religious platitudes as we make excuses instead of learning from our mistakes, engaging the culture and leading the market with a Christian world view that leads through service and knows no surrender—but to Christ!

Principles
& Interest

John Beckett

Principles and Interest

John Beckett, of the R.W. Beckett Corporation, finds business success by applying biblical principles and caring for people.

by Dick Leggatt

The call from ABC headquarters in New York to John Beckett was as unwelcome as it was unsettling. They wanted to do a story featuring his company.

"No way," John first responded. "We're not going to let ABC barge into the R.W. Beckett Corporation, shoot a lot of footage, extract a few sound bites and say whatever they want to say about us on national TV."

Why would ABC be interested anyway in talking with the president of a manufacturing firm in northeastern Ohio that makes components for heating systems? What could John Beckett have possibly done to attract their attention?

Only a year earlier, John had spearheaded an initiative to overturn some proposed guidelines from the Equal Employment Opportunity Commission that would have severely restricted religious freedom in the workplace. His efforts had attracted the attention and support of a number of national print and broadcast media.

Prior to that battle, however, John had already distinguished himself locally and nationally as a principled business leader, centered in his belief that God actually calls people to the world of business as their full-time service to Him. He would go on to write a book based upon his personal experience of integrating his faith with his work.

But all that would come later. For the moment, ABC was calling.

Ready for Prime Time?

Reversing his initial rejection of ABC's request, John agreed to allow a film crew to come to the Beckett Corporation, resulting in prime time coverage on "World News Tonight with Peter Jennings." That evening's topic was an unusual one for the nightly news, companies and business persons like John who use the Bible as a guide to doing business.

During one segment of that broadcast, the correspondent asked John Beckett to state his life's purpose.

"When that clip began, I winced—both from seeing my own face on national TV and wondering what response had made it into the final cut," said John later. "You can imagine how relieved I was to hear the words: 'My main mission in life is to know the will of God and to do it.' Of all the jumbled answers I gave in that high-pressured interview, the correspondent had miraculously extracted my main goal in life in one concise sentence!"

That news segment not only prompted the largest number of favorable calls ever received by an ABC news broadcast, but it also heightened John's commitment to encourage a growing number of business persons to bring their personal beliefs and values into the workplace. This resulted in the publication of his book, *Loving Monday.* "Through *Loving Monday* I wanted to make available to others the lessons I learned in nearly four decades in business," said John. "It's my signature on my life's work to this point."

The Journey—Uphill

National recognition for applying his faith to business, however, would have been the farthest thing from John's mind as he was growing up in Elyria, Ohio, a small industrialized town not far from Cleveland. Raised by loving and principled parents who expected the best of John and his two younger sisters, he had what some might call a "Norman Rockwell" childhood. Among other 'normal' experiences, his family's regular attendance at a local Episcopal church somehow created in John a sense that he might target a career in ministry. "That sounded noble to me," he recalled.

But engineering and business strongly beckoned. His father, Reginald Beckett, an engineer who started a business manufacturing his own specially designed residential oil burner for home heating, had a profound effect upon John's life. When John was accepted at MIT, it seemed clear he would, like his father, head toward a career in business-even though the subtle pressure to "be in ministry" would dog John's vocational decisions for many years.

Ironically, once John arrived as a student at MIT, he found himself repeatedly pestered by classmates who urged him toward a "born again" approach to Christianity. But what they were selling, he wasn't buying. In fact, he dismissed the Bible (and those who tenaciously held to it) as irrelevant to his life and career preparation. That was until he met his future wife, Wendy.

"During our courtship and early marriage, I noticed that Wendy continued to read her well-worn Bible," John recalled. "In spite of her example, I simply was not able to get enthused about this enigmatic book. I would try now and then, dusting off a handsome volume my parents had given me, but it didn't seem relevant. Again and again I would set it aside." This view would eventually change—but not for some years, and not before John would face a number of life-changing challenges.

Soon after his marriage to Wendy in the early sixties, John left a promising position in the aerospace industry to accept his father's invitation to work in his small manufacturing company. The chance to work side-by-side with his dad made the offer one that John simply couldn't refuse. It wasn't long, however, until the trials of life crashed in upon John and Wendy and their fledgling family.

First, their daughter contracted gastroenteritis, a life-threatening condition for infants. Next, Wendy's mother succumbed to a painful battle with cancer. And finally, just one year after inviting John to join him in the business, Reg Beckett was stricken by a fatal heart attack.

"I received the phone call on a cold Saturday morning from the local police," John recalls. "I gasped for breath, my mind in total turmoil as I received the report that Dad had been found slumped over the steering wheel of his car. My only thought was, 'How can this be?'"

This tragedy, along with other difficulties, forced John to recognize his need for spiritual resources far beyond what he presently knew. But not before more trials washed over him.

Just months after his father's passing, as he struggled at age 26 to sustain his newly inherited business, John received yet another phone call, this one at two o'clock in the morning from the local fire department. The

Beckett plant was engulfed in flames. John remembered his thoughts as he arrived on the scene minutes later: "I knew if it went, we were almost certainly out of business for good." Miraculously, the plant survived the fire, but the ordeal was one more challenge drawing John closer to a commitment to the Lord.

"For me, the difficulties I had encountered were gradually opening up insights into the Bible and the ways God works in our lives. Valuable lessons were being forged. In fact, I accepted a challenge at a Christian teaching seminar to read the Bible five minutes each day. At first, it was sheer discipline. But soon I began gleaning insights that affected not only my life, but also my work."

Soon afterward, John's "conversion" took place. As with John Wesley, who at one point found his heart "strangely warmed," John recognized something of great spiritual significance had taken place. Although he could not pinpoint the exact day or hour, he knew he had come into a vital relationship with Jesus Christ.

Called to Business

The spiritual transaction that took place in John caused an old issue to resurface. Despite tremendous success in his growing business pursuits, John's experience of renewal once again raised the question of whether to stay in business or "go into full-time ministry." In John's mind, the question took this form: Is my involvement in business truly my calling, or is it a matter of personal preference? Should I be thinking about some more direct form of ministry?

"I really didn't want to hear that question," John later recounted. "After putting forth my best arguments to the Lord for staying in business, I finally concluded this wasn't a negotiating session. He was probing deep into my heart, examining my motives. After a good deal of soul-searching, I made perhaps the most difficult decision I'd ever made, a decision to release to God my future and all that I owned, including the company."

That step was a watershed in John's life, for he realized God had to be at the center of his business. "I decided to yield everything to Him, including my life's work." In response, God's direction seemed clear, as if He were saying to John: "You are where I want you to be. I have called you to business."

The peace that resulted from finally settling that issue allowed John to move forward in his business career with invigorated confidence. As he began to apply God's principles on the job, his faith grew, providing life-size lessons that have served him well throughout his business career.

Beyond the Bottom Line

John's application of biblical principles to business has been the foundation for growth in the size and scope of his company, and the platform for involvement in a number of other arenas. Today, the Beckett companies are three growing businesses that have diversified into a variety of related product areas, with a total of over 500 employees and about $100 million in annual sales.

But far more important than the numbers is the reality reflected in these companies that God's Word has proved a reliable guide in every business situation, from employee relations to customer service to international marketing decisions. The Bible is the basis for the vision and values that are the very fiber of the family of companies John oversees.

Of the many well-proven business principles upon which the Beckett Corporation is based, three represent Beckett's "core values:" integrity, excellence, and a profound respect for the individual.

John defines integrity as "adherence to a standard of values"—a key concept in his company's mission.

"That which is sound, whole, and complete has integrity. In the biblical use, the term embraces truthfulness, honesty and uprightness—traits found in the person described in Psalm 15, who 'swears to his own hurt and does not change.' I picture someone who agrees on a handshake to sell a piece of property for a certain sum. The next day another person offers more money. The person of integrity honors the prior commitment, even though backing out would bring greater profit."

John describes excellence as that which reflects the best of God's creation. "Whenever something bears the mark of God's kingdom, it will be excellent. We will never fully duplicate the perfection of the heavenly realm, but by aligning ourselves with God's ambassador to earth, Jesus Christ, we can certainly emulate it. Ultimately, excellence is defined not by a product or a process but by a Person."

One of the most compelling characteristics of a biblically focused business is the way employees are regarded and treated,centered in a profound respect for the individual. This dimension stood out the strongest when the ABC correspondent asked John Beckett, "What makes your company different from the one down the street?"

The news segment highlighted some of the practices within the company that reflect a commitment to the dignity and intrinsic worth of the individual—policies such as John's personal involvement in the hiring process, decisions to allow mothers with newborns to stay home with them for an extended period, or company subsidies to families who adopt children.

According to John, "The important thing is to view people the way God does. In Genesis we read that God formed men and women in his own image and likeness. When I really saw this, it changed the way I viewed not only myself but other people. I concluded I must place a high value on each person and never look down on another, regardless of his or her station or situation in life. To apply this, employees must be provided a dignified and supportive work environment where they are viewed as valued, important, worthy. They bear God's own image. If they are of infinite worth in his eyes, they certainly deserve no less from us than our profound respect."

After all, he reasons, "We are salt. We are light. We are God's ambassadors, in business or wherever we are, and to everyone with whom He brings us in contact." John's overriding conviction is that people who carry a vision for business based upon biblical principles will inevitably make an impact on the world around them—especially the world of business.

Dick Leggatt, a former Editor of New Wine Magazine, is Vice President of the Ohio Roundtable, a grassroots public policy organization. He and his wife, Cindi, have four children and reside in Elyria, Ohio.

Leadership
& Management

Equipping
Others

John Maxwell

Equipping Others to Lead

Leadership expert and motivational speaker John Maxwell knows that you can't grow beyond the people around you, so he is equipping everyone around him

by Brian Mast

Moving up the corporate ladder is the goal of almost every businessman. With this upward mobility comes an expected increase in pay and a new title. Accompanying this promotion is the unavoidable increase in responsibility. For many, this is the "price" of leadership, not realizing what they have just gained could be the catalyst that launches them past their wildest expectations. On average, however, most fail to see the potential in their responsibility, so they wander (and wonder) aimlessly up the corporate ladder.

Not John Maxwell! As the founder of INJOY in 1985, a parent organization whose sole purpose is to develop leaders, he has seen far too much change, excitement and growth from well-trained leaders to ever go back to the ways of visionless leadership. He has been a part of literally thousands of individual's lives being changed as they rise up and become leaders of excellence and integrity.

Through seminars and conferences held across North America and high quality resources, including books, audio cassette kits, monthly tape subscriptions and instructional videos, leaders are beginning to take advantage of the responsibility they have been given. They learn that as they become better communicators, encouragers and motivators, their staff will not only enjoy work and produce more, they will be loyal to the leadership.

Dick Peterson, president of INJOY, Inc., left his job of over 20 years with IBM because he believed in Maxwell and his vision to help grow pastors and businessmen. The goal of INJOY, Inc. is to develop leaders of excellence and integrity by providing the finest resources and training for personal and professional growth. Peterson has remained loyal and committed to Maxwell for the past 18 years, to the benefit of everyone involved. "Making a positive impact in a person's life is fulfilling," Peterson explains, as is the "rare opportunity to combine business skills in a ministry environment."

Leadership is Everything

Several years ago, while pastoring a church in Lancaster, Ohio, Maxwell came to the realization that good leadership was more than important_it was indispensable! He recognized that both the ability to minister and the effectiveness of any organization increases only when its leaders positively develop their leadership abilities. In short, the better the leader, the better the business. This understanding has been a driving force behind Maxwell's focus and dedication to teaching leadership principles for the past 23 years.

Today, businesses like Sam's Club, Wal-Mart, Home Interiors, Mary Kay, Inc., the Prince Corporation, and others, are benefiting from Maxwell's leadership training programs. "I help them train leaders in their organizations," Maxwell explains. "By training a leader you have developed the potential of an organization." Success in the business is of course important, but it is not the motivating factor in training other leaders to lead properly. Maxwell points out, "I work hard to help them grow people instead of growing the company. If you grow the company without growing the person, the individual in that position will sabotage the company sooner or later."

Businesses that look at the bottom line as being merely financial are missing the point. Maxwell states, "Money has nothing to do with success_adding value does. You cannot equate adding value with dollars." He goes on to explain, "The values I have in life are my core principles that guide me. If my values are good, they add value to people. If my values are bad, they rob people of value. I am either depleting or replenishing based on what my values are, simply because I'm going to transfer them."

By putting people first and allowing them to, for example, operate in an area that matches their gifting or communicate more freely with an attentive boss, Maxwell has found company growth to be a natural outcome. The bottom line for increased growth, he notes, is that "you can't grow beyond the people you have around you; they are your biggest asset or your biggest liability."

Better leadership not only sounds good to employees, but it also makes sense (in terms of dollars and cents!) to employers. "Leaders influence people," Maxwell says, "which in turn generates momentum and morale." He has found that organizations with high morale usually have good leaders. Common sense would add that businesses and ministries with high morale and good leaders will also generate good returns on their products or efforts. Truly a win-win situation.

The cry for good quality leadership, Maxwell has found, is within every individual and business. Everyone either feels the effect of poor leadership or enjoys the results of good leadership. No matter how you figure it, leadership is central in the equation for growth among organizations. This is evident by the fact that over 150,000 people listen to the monthly tapes he produces for his INJOY Life Club (for the church world) and Maximum Impact Club (for the business world).

To be able to produce two new tapes a month on leadership and a quarterly newsletter, Maxwell spends hours "reading, studying, learning, filing, and gleaning." This, he adds, "is the freshness of leadership" that enables their leadership teachings to remain on the cutting edge.

Leaders Are Led

John C. Maxwell, born in 1947 in Garden City, Michigan, was the second of three children. He grew up around the Bible and church and would even play "church" while other children played "school." He accepted Christ into his life at age three and when he was 17 he reaffirmed his commitment while at a youth camp.

Maxwell credits his parents for being highly influential in forming his character and outlook on life. Besides being a good leader and keeping the home disciplined, his father was a pastor of a growing church, district superintendent and Bible college president and went on to help plant 40 churches. As a result, Maxwell recalls, "leadership came naturally to me," as did church planting and church growth. His mother, similarly, had a large impact on his life. She was a "compassionate listener," he explains, which in turn "fostered in me a great sense of security and self-esteem."

At an early age, Maxwell knew he would some day be a preacher. From high school he went directly to Bible college and received his Bachelor's Degree in 1969. The month he graduated he also married Margaret Porter, went on a honeymoon and moved to Hillham, Indiana, where he took his first position as a senior pastor.

While pastoring in Hillham, Maxwell's character was put to the test. God revealed to him that he had been a "people pleaser" up to that point in his ministry—and it must change! Maxwell immediately abandoned his pursuit of popularity and dedicated himself wholeheartedly to what he calls, "a genuine service to God."

From Hillham, Indiana, Maxwell moved to Lancaster, Ohio, having seen his church grow from a congregation of three to three hundred in a matter of three years. While in Lancaster, Maxwell faced his second challenge, this time in the area of evangelism. Maxwell told his congregation that he would attempt to lead 200 people to Christ outside of his pulpit ministry in the coming year. Though he missed his goal, Maxwell explains (he succeeded in helping 186 make commitments), "it marked a watershed in my ministry and a lifelong commitment to evangelism."

It was also in Lancaster as Senior Pastor of Faith Memorial Church that Maxwell realized the importance of leadership with regards to ministry and the effectiveness of an organization. This revelation marked the beginning of his lifelong calling to instruction and teaching in the area of leadership. Also during this time he sensed that God was calling him into a ministry of service to pastors.

Soon, pastors were inviting him to teach on how to effectively grow their churches. In 1980, after eight years of pastoring and seeing his church grow from 400 to 1,300, he stepped out of the position of pastor and into the position of Executive Director of Evangelism at the Wesleyan World Headquarters in Anderson, Indiana. During the 18 months there, he developed a whole-church ministry model that focused on prayer, evangelism, discipleship and encouragement. As a result, each of the 15 churches he assisted doubled in size.

Maxwell's desire was to help pastors from not just one denomination, but from many. In 1981 he was asked to pastor the Skyline Wesleyan Church in San Diego, California, and he accepted, with the condition that he be allowed to continue mentoring and assisting other pastors as he led his own congregation. As the need for training and development in the area of leadership became more apparent, Maxwell founded a company called INJOY and created the INJOY Life Club, a monthly leadership equipping tape taught to Maxwell's church staff and sent out to pastors around the country.

The leadership tapes were received with such enthusiasm that the number of subscriptions quickly increased from hundreds to over ten thousand. The pastors' desire for help was far greater than Maxwell had imagined, and his all-volunteer company soon required full-time paid staff members.

In 1992, Maxwell took his congregation through the process of raising funds to relocate the church. The experience opened his eyes to see another viable ministry to fellow pastors, and INJOY Stewardship Services (ISS) was born. ISS was designed to help pastors teach biblical stewardship and raise money in their churches to build, relocate and retire debt. Under Dave Sutherland's leadership, within three years it became the second largest company of its type in the world. The next year, a Hispanic division was also formed to help Spanish-speaking churches raise funds.

Then, in 1995, after leading Skyline for 14 years and seeing his congregation increase three-fold, Maxwell resigned his position as senior pastor to pursue the ever-expanding opportunities of INJOY.

The Acid Test

The real test of a motivational speaker is to see what his own staff has to say about him. We asked Linda Eggers, Assistant to John Maxwell, how she felt about her boss. She candidly said, "I am fortunate to work with someone who breathes and lives by the principles he teaches." Apparently, the principles he teaches actually work, for she concludes, "I feel I'm a full partner in all he does," and adds, "I work for the 'perfect' boss."

Leaders Lead

Today, John Maxwell is in great demand as a motivational speaker and teacher. An estimated one million people are touched every year through seminars, speaking engagements, audio and video resources and books. His passion continues to be helping pastors develop their leadership skills, though he does impact the business world by speaking to large groups of business leaders, both in person and via his monthly tapes.

To increase the realm of influence, Maxwell founded a non-profit organization called EQUIP (Encouraging Qualities Undeveloped In People), which offers leadership training and material to international ministry organizations, academic institutions and urban communities. EQUIP, under the leadership of Ron McManus, recently trained 5,000 national pastors and leaders in India and Indonesia. Over a thousand churches in unreached villages are expected to result from EQUIP's impact in these nations.

Maxwell has not arrived at the peak of his career. He is just beginning. His mission, in a nutshell, is to "find ten people more gifted than myself and add value to their life. Today I have seven. I want to develop a team of 100 people around me to accomplish my vision. I want to assist one thousand pastors in building a church of a thousand in America. I developed a conference strategy for this purpose. I would like ten thousand people called to the ministry under me. I want to train one hundred thousand people for leadership. I want to raise up one million prayer partners for pastors across America and I hope to equip ten million people in my lifetime."

Maxwell has more vision than he can handle in his own strength, which is precisely the point. He is embarking on a mission so large that only God can do it, thus leaving undeniable evidence of God's power and that God alone is worthy to be glorified.

Questions and Answers

Q: What made you leave the ministry to pursue INJOY?

A: I didn't (leave the ministry). I left the local church. More people have received Christ since I've been out the pulpit than when I was in the pulpit. I wanted to have a lasting impact by helping people go to a new level.

Q: What happened to the staff you had in San
        Diego and how many do you have now?
A: When I moved from San Diego to Atlanta,
        my key people followed. I moved 38
        families (57 employees) and I have a little
        over a hundred on staff now.

Q: You want to find ten people and add to
        their lives. How do you distinguish those
        individuals from the rest?
A: They have a greater potential to do
        something for God than I do. It's a serving
        role and God brings those people to me.
        Jim Dornan (featured in the May issue of
        (The Christian Businessman) is one due
        to his commitment to God in the business
        community. I provide them with books I
        believe they should read. I also offer
        individual consultation, provide leadership
        and serve as a friend.

Your Need to Lead

by Joe D. Batten

Leadership is for those who are in the front—leading. And if you lead, you will be followed.

Most of our current leadership vocabulary is dated. I maintain that the following phrases are oxymoronic:

Directive-leadership
Values-driven leadership
Running an organization

As we have seen, leadership and top quality don't exist without followers. And followers are not driven; they are pulled. They are not pushed; they are led! They are not diminished; they are enhanced!

Do you feel:

Pushed or led by your values?
Pushed or led by your motives?
Driven or pulled by your vision?
Driven or equipped by data?

Do you feel more stimulated and responsive when:

You are told rather than asked?
You are compressed rather than stretched?
You are running rather than leading an operation?
Your weaknesses are emphasized and your
strengths ignored?

Are your vision and values behind you—pushing you?
Or are your vision and values ahead of you—pulling you?
Charles Garfield (1986) says, "No matter which measure
of worth predominates in any given person, when all else
is said and done, the force with the strongest pull toward
high achievement concerns quality, principle and
intrinsic value."

What would happen to a spacecraft that had
tremendous thrust, but no orbit or trajectory plotted? What
happens to your team members if you give them lots of
push, thrust, and pressure without clear and stretching
expectations and guidelines? The answer is pretty
obvious.

People often respond that these are only words, only
semantics, and how important are words? In actuality,
we ultimately become what we say! Words are the only
tools we possess. How can computer software be
developed without words? What can fax machines
transmit that is not created by, interpreted by, and acted
on except words? How can lasers be created and used
without words? How can new concepts of quality we
created with words? Here is a preliminary list of truly
expective leadership words and their directive or driven
counterparts.

Leadership & Management

Expective Words

Expect. To look forward; to anticipate; to consider probable or certain.

Elicit. To call forth or bring out a response, to draw forth; to evoke; to bring out something latent.

Motivation. Motive-action; action guided and pulled by motive-action to achieve motive; motive-led

Pull. A force that attracts, compels, or influences; magnetic force; to seek to obtain by making one's wants known. To call on for a response.

Ask. To call for; to seek; to invite; to make a request.

Stretch. To extend in length; to pull taut; reach or continue from one point to another; search for a better way.

Directive Words

Direct. To impel an authoritative instrument forward.

Drive or Driven. Having a compulsive or urgent quality; applying force to push.

Congest. To concentrate in a small or narrow space; to become congested.

Push. A physical force steadily applied in a direction away from the body exerting it.

Tell. To give utterance to; to assure emphatically.

Compress. To reduce in size or volume as if by squeezing; flatten; to make inert.

143

Some key words and phrases for the tough-minded leadership lexicon include:

Expect	Listen	Hear
Ask	Market-led	Possibilities
Customer-led	Expand	Renewal
Request	Enhance	Empowerment
Evoke	Unfold	Empathic
Compete (with self)	Blossom	Build
Commitment	Care	Coach
Consistency	Communication	Vulnerability
Vitality	Vision	Value-led
Resilient	Serve	Positive stress
Responsibility	Significance	Synergy
Symbiosis	Strength bank	Respect
Quality	Possibility teams	Passion
Help	Excellence	Integrity
Stretch	Counsel (not advice)	

The creative deployment of strengths.
Strengths enhancement.
Performance is all that matters.
Attitude is everything.
A system of expective leadership.
Reverse the G-forces.
Relish and embrace change.
Above all—integrity
We are transformed by the renewal of our minds
Learn, learn, learn.

Joe D. Batten is Chairman and CEO of the consulting firm of Batten, Batten, Hudson & Swab, Inc. Excerpted with permission, from Building A Total Quality Culture, Joe D. Batten, Crisp Publications, Inc. (1992). His other recent books include: The Master Motivator, Tough-Minded Leadership and The Leadership Principles of Jesus. Visit his Web Site at: www.daretolive.com

PRESENTATION SKILLS

by Tony Jeary
Mr. Presentation™

An Undiscovered Secret To Success

What many people fail to recognize is this: Whenever you are talking to others, you are making a presentation of sorts and you are being judged.

We may not like that, but it is true. We might not be consciously aware of how intently we study others when they are addressing us. We do it automatically and very subtly. We are aware of eye contact, firmness of grip, ability to speak clearly and distinctly and many other things that go into the overall total opinion we are making about that person. I believe every individual should make a dedicated effort to improve and develop their presentation and communication skills. This principle has a vital application for Christian business people who want to be a effective witness for Christ in the business community.

To improve your presentation and communication skills, there are 7 Foundational Secrets™ that need to be followed. The highlights are as follows:

The 7 Foundational Secrets™ to Great Presentations

Secret #1: The Funneling Process. This is a process that helps you uncover and clarify the real objectives of your talk. You should know clearly who your audience is, and what actions you want them to take as a result of hearing your message. If you can't identify the clear objectives, you won't be able to accomplish them very easy. There are specific steps you can take to process what you know about your audience and use that information to design, create and deliver a more effective message. Learning this skill is the first step in becoming a more effective presenter and communicator.

Secret #2: Four Subconscious Tensions. Every audience (even an audience of one) has four stress factors that potentially can inhibit your presentation. The first is tension between themselves and others (listeners). The second is tension between themselves and the speaker/presenter (you). The third tension exists between themselves and any materials being used. Lastly, the fourth tension is between themselves and the physical environment of the presentation. Effective presenters know to diffuse these tensions so that people can really hear your message.

Secret #3: Trust-Transference. Without trust it is hard to get buy-in. An effective presenter must know how to accomplish what I call 'trust-transference' to create a higher level of acceptance for their ideas and words.

Secret #4: Business Entertainment.™ If your audience isn't captivated, you can't be assured of their full attention. Without their attention you can't be very effective. People like to have fun, and they are more likely to respond favorably when they are having fun.

Secret #5: Verbal Surveying. With this skill you will be able to get useful feedback during your entire presentation. It involves learning how to simply ask your audience some critical questions as you speak with them. Their answers will help you better direct your presentation and insure your message is on target for them.

When everything else is equal, the ability to effectively present and communicate your ideas is the greatest single factor in success!

Secret #6: Targeted Polling. This skill helps you decrease nervousness. It is more effectively used in groups because it requires you to recruit and establish advocates from those who are attending your presentation. Many presenters miss the opportunity to talk one-on-one with audience members. Doing this before your presentation, or during breaks helps reduce audience tension, nervousness and gives you a better understanding of what your audience members are really feeling, needing and wanting.

Secret #7: Audience Closure. Proper closure means that you don't overwhelm them with too much information before you go on to the next point or complete your talk. People can only absorb so much. As a presenter, you need to help them by giving many mini-summaries throughout your talk.

Because people form opinions of us by the way we conduct ourselves, it is certain that we are judged on our ability to present and communicate our ideas. Remember, whatever the message, when it is transmitted clearly and effectively, the possibility that others will accept the message is much greater.

Tony Jeary, known by many of his clients as Mr. Presentation ™, is an authority on presentation skills. He is the author of Inspire Any Audience (Honor, 1997) book, video, and audio courses, from which a portion of this article originated. He also serves as the CEO of High Performance Resources, an international learning and performance company. He can be reached at 1-877-2-INSPIRE *or by* E-Mail at MrPresentation@MrPresentation.com

Continuing His
Father's Legacy

Dick DeVos

CONTINUING HIS FATHERS LEGACY

With a clear vision to lead a multi-billion dollar company into the 21st century, Dick DeVos firmly grasped the baton passed to him from the hand of his ailing father.

by Rob Dilbone

Rich DeVos lay in a hospital bed near death awaiting heart surgery. Less than a week before the planned public announcement of his son's succession to the Amway presidency, Rich DeVos suffered a severe heart attack. What should have been a time of deep satisfaction after years of preparation and planning had been reduced to a hastened act of necessity. It was a very challenging time," recalls Dick, "but my father made it clear to me that the plan was set, and his physical condition only reinforced his desire for that plan to proceed."

Dick DeVos began his career with the Amway corporation when he was 12, pulling weeds out in front of the company's office building. He made 35 cents an hour that summer and could not have imagined that 25 years later he would lead the international multi-billion dollar corporation. While some might think it was a forgone conclusion that the president's eldest son would one day take his father's place, the reality was quite different.

Job Training

Realizing that their children might potentially lead their company, co-founders Rich DeVos and Jay Van

Andel developed what they referred to as a "training program" through which their children could be properly prepared for positions of leadership in the event they earned them. Each was asked to work in virtually every area of the business. "It was a five year program that took me six years to complete," Dick says with a smile. "We did everything from loading trucks, working the production lines, research and development, marketing, accounting and working as distributors. We routinely went into a department and filled in for staff when they needed us."

Dick completed his training and was offered a position heading up what was then a small segment of Amway: the international market. International sales soared from 10-15 percent to over one half of Amway's total sales volume through Dick's leadership. He also spent several years expanding the foreign market from 11 to 18 countries. Today Amway receives 70 percent of its sales from outside the United States. "What is exciting," he says, "is that the vast majority of those goods are manufactured in the US and exported to our foreign consumers."

After six years in the international division, Dick decided to leave Amway and pursue outside business interests. "I left at a time when most people felt I was the heir apparent to my father and the presidency," says Dick. "My father and mother totally supported the decision and understood the rationale for it...they were very encouraging." Dick and his wife Betsy established their own business interests by investing in and buying a variety of companies, many of which they are still involved in today.

Early Preparation

Dick remembers that his formative years were "quite normal." His parents provided a Christ-centered home while his father was busy building a small business in the basement. "I can still remember the office downstairs," says Dick, whose parents proved to be great role models. "The most defining characteristic of our family was that my father and mother lived at home what they talked about in public. There was absolute consistency between what they said and the way they lived."

Despite a growing family and business, the DeVoses took seriously the responsibility of rearing their four children with a work ethic. "Our parents encouraged us to fully develop and explore the abilities God gave us as kids," Dick explains. "They urged us to go out and do what we could do and be the best we could be with whatever talents were given."

The Fabric of Business

Dick believes that his personal faith must be a vital part of his daily business. He says, "It really orients me philosophically toward right and wrong. It comes in for me not in the tactical sense, but in the strategic sense." This foundation of faith causes him to see others in a different light. "Other people are equally created as you are by God and therefore they are special," he notes. "We must view people as much more than a commodity." Faith also defines Dick's management style. "You must respect people," he explains, "you encourage them, you treat them with dignity, you treat them openly and fairly. You respect their family life by doing things to allow them to return to their families whenever possible."

Dick also believes that as a Christian you must be an example to others in the workplace by upholding a standard of righteousness. A good friend and a member of his accountability group said, "As a Christian, there are certain arrows in your quiver of potential tactics and approaches to business that you simply cannot use." To that Dick adds, "The arrows are there, but you just cannot use them as a Christian. You cannot use intimidation, bribery or deceit, so you must reach into your quiver and find things you can use. And there are plenty of arrows you can use as a Christian to be successful and active business. When other people look at how I conduct the affairs of my business, do they see it as a reflection of my faith or do they see it as contrary to it? If it is contrary, I have a problem. I hope and pray that others see my conduct as a positive reflection of my faith."

Family Life Today

Today Dick and Betsy have four children of their own, two boys and two girls. The DeVoses began a home schooling program for two of their children, enabling them to experience some fascinating events on the road. One memorable family trip included stops in Japan, Hong Kong, India, the Philippines, Thailand and Vietnam. "We celebrated Easter Sunday with a small international group of Christians right in the middle of Hanoi," says Dick, "It was a stunning contrast and a fascinating experience I will never forget."

Dick doesn't have typical days, but he tries to keep life as normal as possible for the kids. He is usually up early, exercises regularly and spends a few minutes with the kids to "connect a little bit" before school. Dick's schedule includes a steady contingent of travel, but he makes it a point to return home as quickly as he can. "I try to get home...even if it is very late so I can be there in the morning for my family," says Dick.

Betsy is also in a demanding, high profile position as the chair of the Michigan Republican Party. "We balance between our schedules," says Dick, "and we always block off Sunday as our day of rest and worship, whether we are in or out of town."

Priorities and Principles

One of Dick's business priorities is to increase communication of the Amway vision. "We are still at times a misunderstood organization," he says. "Many do not understand direct selling and the ability therein to penetrate a market." Amway has penetrated the foreign markets of many countries with the American dream of opportunity. The business has enjoyed tremendous success in Japan, for example, where there are over a million distributors. Poland, Hungary, Malaysia, Thailand and the Philippines are also opening their doors to the Amway business opportunity. Amway is literally handing over the keys to free enterprise-a vehicle they have never driven. "They are the ones who must turn the keys," Dick insists. "We are not a social welfare organization. It involves their effort. They must buckle down and do the things necessary to make their business successful."

Dick is passionate about being able to offer the same freedom of opportunity that Americans have to those in other nations. In his recent book, *Rediscovering American Values: The Foundations of Our Freedom* for the 21st Century (Dutton, 1997), Dick offers a rare look into the values that champion the free enterprise system. Dick shares accounts of both the famous and the obscure, who have successfully met life's challenges by applying values like honesty, courage and accountability.

The DeVoses are careful to maintain who they in countries where the Christian population is minimal. "It is a very interesting paradox because some people feel that to be accepted by others you have to give up what you believe. I don't think that at all. I feel you must stand up and state clearly what you believe and then be willing to extend and respect that same right in to others. That doesn't mean you have to compromise your beliefs, but it does mean you conduct yourself in a different way than if you had no regard for the beliefs of others. This has been a good approach for us when we travel overseas and the same philosophy has been a very successful approach for us in the Amway business," Dick says.

Currently, Amway Corporation and its two sister companies, Amway Japan and Amway Asia Pacific, are projected to have $10 billion in sales in the near future. But Dick knows Amway is capable of doing even more. He is well prepared to lead Amway into a larger presence in the global marketplace. Dick DeVos is a man who knows who he is, what he needs to do to succeed, and where he is going. His father, having recovered well from heart transplant surgery in Europe, and everyone associated with the Amway Corporation can be confident in the leadership that will take them into the next century.

To all businessman: comments from Dick DeVos

Businessmen must seek out success in every area of their lives. "I let businessmen know that it can be done," says Dick. "I have seen it in my own family-where my father was a model of true success in every dimension including his Christian witness. My father-in-law also was a tremendous example of a man who successfully raised a family, built a thriving business and was highly regarded within his community as a man of faith.

Dick also says that businessmen, by nature, use money as a score keeping system. "Unfortunately, we tend too quickly to carry that over into other areas of our lives. But money should never be the measure within our families, our relationships or within our spiritual life."

A friend and confidant told Dick one day, "As a Christian, there are certain arrows in your quiver of potential tactics and approaches to business that you simply cannot use." Dick adds, "The arrows are there, but you just cannot use them as a Christian. You cannot use intimidation, bribery or deceit, so you must reach into your quiver and find things you can use. And there are plenty of arrows you can use as a Christian to be successful and active in business. When other people look at how I conduct the affairs of my business, do they see it as a reflection of my faith or do they see it as contrary to it? If it is contrary, I have a problem. I hope and pray that others see my conduct as a positive reinforcement of my faith."

HOW TO ORDER
YOUR PRIORITIES

by Patrick Morley

Priorities, like promises,
need to be kept

Once we invited Bill Walton, co-founder of Holiday Inn who experienced a late-in-life conversion, to speak at an outreach dinner. As it happened, our Bible study was meeting the next meeting so I invited Mr. Walton.

The next morning after our Bible study, a group or about eight men, ages 30 to 45 each spent two or three minutes describing where they were on their spiritual pilgrimages.

As each successful man shared, I noticed Mr. Walton, a father of four, becoming more an more fidgety. Finally, it was his turn to speak. He said, "It is true that I helped to build a great corporation. But to do so I arrived at the office every morning by seven and rarely got home before ten o'clock at night," His brow furrowed, his shoulders drooped, and his lip quivered as had added, "I never saw a single little league baseball game."

What are Priorities?

Mr. Walton would have us know that men who fail usually fail because they didn't manage their priorities.

The dictionary says that a "priority" is something to which we give precedence because of its urgency or importance. To "prioritize" means to arrange in order of importance.

Priorities, then, are "pre-decisions" we make to decide in advance what we will give ourselves to. When we set priorities we are literally writing history in advance.

Priorities become a grid to help us distinguish opportunity from distraction. They are filters throughout which we can sift daily decisions to make sure we keep on track. When we wet priorities in advance it reduces the pressure we feel when we must make decisions under fire.

The Example of Jesus

Jesus made decisions based on his priorities. One morning after a tiring night, Jesus went to have some time to himself. It was not to be...

At daybreak Jesus went out to a solitary place. The people came to where he was and tried to keep him from leaving them. But he said, "I must preach the good news of the kingdom of God to the other towns also, because that is why I was sent" (Luke 4:42-44).

Notice three things. First, people tried to keep Jesus from leaving. Perhaps they appealed to his compassion. The better job you do, the more people will ask you to do . Without intending to , people will ask you to do things that meet their needs, but don't necessarily match your priorities.

Second, Jesus knew his purpose. He said, "I must preach the good news...because that is why I was sent." His purpose determined his priorities. He did not let the emotion of the moment could hid judgement. Since he decided n advance what he should do, he was not distracted.

Third, Jesus did what he was called to do. The pressure to do that which is good but not best has put many wagons in the ditch. There is one great rule for priority living we glean from the example of Jesus: make decisions on the basis of your priorities, not your pressures.

How to Prioritize

No man can do everything. Choices must be made. How can priorities help us make choices about how we invest our limited time and money?

Triage is the military technique of deciding how to prioritize treatment of wounded soldiers when a wave of new casualties swamps the capacity of the medic unit. The helicopters bring back three groups of wounded soldiers:

> Those who will die no matter what is done.
> Those who will live even if treatment is delayed.
> Those who will live only if given immediate treatment.

Can you guess the order of treatment? For our personal decision-making we should conduct a little civilian triage:

Who can't live without you, or you without them?

Who would you help if you didn't have to neglect group "a?"—who are those who will be fine with or without you?

Why is it that we often give the most of our time to those who care about us the least, and the least of our time to those who care about us the most? That's why we should decide in advance what our priorities ought to be, prioritizing everything on the basis of who will cry at our funeral.

Never do anything someone else can do.

Many years ago I decided I would only do things I do well. That served a good purpose, because it kept me in my areas of competence. However, I have also realized that simply because I do something well doesn't mean it's the best use of my time.

Since then I've added a "part two." I also don't do anything if someone else can also do it. Since I write and prepare messages at my home office, this means if I need a photocopy I get up a make it at my copy machine. But when I am at the ministry office I have someone else make it. This principle frees us unusually large amounts of time. Try it (but don't tell your wife to take out the trash instead of you—it really is something only you can do for reasons that should be obvious!)

Distinguish opportunity from distraction. Many times distractions come disguised as opportunities.

Unless we have thought through who we are, what our lives are all about, and what's important to us, we will not have the focus to choose the best. Al Ries says that focus is the art of exclusion. A great secret of priority living is to have so thought through your life that deciding what to include and excluded becomes second nature.

Recognize the difference between a good idea and a God idea

We are naturally inclined to act on the impulse of a good idea. But sometimes good ideas get in the way of God ideas. Peter wanted to build three shelters for Moses, Elijah and Jesus at the transfiguration. The Bible says, "that while he (Peter) was still speaking, God spoke (Matthew 17:5)." In other words, Peter's good idea was so impetuous that God literally interrupted Peter—"while he was still speaking."

Prayer removes the impulse of the good idea born of human ingenuity but not of God. Pray, then plan. It is the habit of a man who would distinguish between good and God.

Areas to Prioritize

Every one must take personal responsibility for his private life and set priorities in five areas: his relationship with God, his relationship with his wife, his relationship with his children, his finances, and his health (including leisure and rest). No one else will, or can, do this for you. Also a man must set priorities for his work and his personal ministry.

Patrick Morley is a business leader, men's author, and speaker. He is Chairman and CEO of Man in the Mirror, a ministry which conducts church-sponsored men's events. Patrick has been used to help men think more deeply about their lives, to be reconciled with Christ, and to be equipped to have a larger impact on the world. To contact Man in the Mirror, write 154 Wilshire Blvd., Casselberry, FL 32707, or call: 407-331-0095.

The Law of
Explosive Growth

by John Maxwell

To add growth, lead followers
—to multiply, lead leaders

In 1984 at age 22, John Schnatter started his own business. He began selling pizzas out of a converted broom closet at Mick's Tavern, a lounge that was co-owned by his father. Although he was just a kid, he had a tremendous amount of vision, drive and energy—enough to make his tiny pizza stand into a success. the next year, he opened his first store next door to Mick's in Jeffersonville, Indiana. He named the place Papa John's. For the next several years, Schnatter worked hard to build the company. In time, he opened additional stores, and later he began selling franchises. By the beginning of 1991, he had 46 stores. That in itself is a success story. But what happened during the next couple of years is even better.

In 1991 and 1992, Papa John's turned a huge corner. By the end of 1991, the number of stores more than doubled to 110 units. By the end of 1992, they had doubled again to 220. And the growth has continued dramatically. In early 1992, that number surpassed 1,600. What made the company suddenly experience such an incredible period of rapid expansion? The answer can be found in the Law of Explosive Growth.

Schnatter had always hired good people for his staff, but in the early years he was really the sole leader and primary driving force behind the business's success. Back in the 1980s, he didn't dedicate much time to developing other strong leaders. "It's taking a lot of growing on my part," says Schnatter of Papa John's success. "Between 26 and 32 [years old], the hardest thing was that a lot of [people needed coaching, and I was so busy developing myself, trying to get myself to the next level, I didn't develop those people. As a result, I lost them. It's my job to build the people who are going to build the company. That's going to be much harder for me than the first 1,200 stores." [1]

The Key to Growth

In the early 1990s, Schnatter began thinking about what it would take to really grow the company. The key was leadership. He had already begun to grow as a leader personally. His having made significant progress in his leadership development was opening the door for him to attract better leaders to the company and to give them the time they needed. That's when he started recruiting some of the people who currently lead the company, including Wade Oney, now the company's C.O.O. Wade had worked for Domino's Pizza for fourteen years, and John believed he was one of the reasons that company had been so successful. When Wade left Domino's, John immediately asked him to be part of the Papa John Pizza team.

Schnatter had already built a company capable of creating a taste-tempting pizza—and earning a healthy profit in the process. (Their per-store sales average is higher than that of Pizza Hut, Domino's or Little Ceasar's.) Their goal was to build a bigger company. Together, they started talking about what it would take to be capable of opening four hundred new restaurants a year. And that's when they focused their attention on developing leaders so that they could take the company to the next level. Says Oney, "The reason we're successful in the marketplace is our focus on quality and our desire to keep things simple. The reason we're successful as a company is our good people."

Since the early 1990s, Schnatter and Oney have developed a top-rate team of leaders who are helping the company experience explosive growth, people such as Blaine Hurst, Papa John's president and vice chairman; Durcilla "Dru" Milby, the CFO; Robert Waddell, president of Papa John's Food Service; and Hart Boesel, who heads up franchise operations.

Papa John's growth has been phenomenal in an industry that was thought to be glutted with competitors a decade ago. In 1997, they opened more than 350 new restaurants. In 1998, they expected the number to be more than 400. And they are also implementing plans to launch Papa John's internationally. They don't plan to stop growing until they are the largest seller of pizza in the world.

"The challenge now," explains Oney, "is developing the next leaders. The company's in great shape financially. [Acquiring] real estate is always a battle, but we can succeed there. And the economy is never a deterrent when you offer customers a good value. The key is to develop leaders. You do that by building up people."

Leader's Math brings Explosive Growth

John Schnatter and Wade Oney have succeeded because they have practiced the Law of Explosive Growth. Any leader who does that makes the shift from follower's math to what I call leader's math. Here's how it works. Leaders who develop followers grow their organization only one persona at a time. But leaders who develop leaders multiply their growth, because for every leader they develop, they also receive all of that leader's followers. Add ten followers to your organization, and you have the power of ten people. Add ten leaders to your organization, and you have the power of ten leaders times all the followers and leaders they influence. That's the difference between addition and multiplication. It's like growing your organization by teams instead of by individuals. The better the leaders you develop, the greater the quality and quantity of followers.

To go to the highest level, you have to develop leaders of leaders. My friend Dale Galloway asserts, some leaders want to make followers. I want to make leaders. not only do I want to make leaders, but I want to make leaders of leaders. And then leaders of leaders of leaders." Once you are able to follow that pattern, there is almost no limit to the growth of your organization. That's why I say to add growth, leaders followers, but to multiply growth, lead leaders. That's the Law of Explosive Growth.

Dr. John Maxwell has been called "America's Expert on Leadership." Author of more than twenty books and a highly sought-after speaker, John is the founder of INJOY, Inc., a company that seeks to develop leadership potential in every aspect of a person's life. He resides in Atlanta, Georgia. Reprinted by permission of Thomas Nelson Publishers. From the book, The 21 Irrefutable Laws of Leadership. Copyright © 1998, John Maxwell.

[1]. Rajan Chaudhry, "Dough Boy," Chain Leader, April 1997.

You're Like A Teabag

by John Mason

Not Worth Much 'Til You've
Been Through Some Hot Water

Have you ever failed or made a mistake? If you have, then this nugget is for you. The fact that you've failed is proof that you're not finished. Failures and mistakes can be a bridge, not a barricade, to success.

Psalms 37:23-24 says, "The steps of a good man are ordered by the Lord: and he delighteth in his way, he shall not be utterly cast down: for the Lord uphodeth him with his hand." Failure may look like a fact, but it's just an opinion. Successful people believe that mistakes are just feedback. It's not how far you fall but how high you bounce back that makes all the difference.

Theodore Roosevelt said, "Far better it is to dare mighty things, to win glorious triumphs, even though checkered by failure than to rank with those poor spirits who neither enjoy much nor suffer much because they live in the great twilight that knows not victory or defeat." One of the riskiest things you can do in life is to take too many precautions and never have any failures or mistakes. Failure is the opportunity to start over more intelligently.

No one ever achieved worthwhile success without, at one time or another, teetering on the edge of disaster. If you have tried to do something and failed, you are vastly better off than if you had tried to do nothing and succeeded. The person who never makes a mistake must get awfully tired doing nothing. If you're not making mistakes, you're not risking enough.

Vernon Sanders says, "Experience is a hard teacher because she gives the test first, the lesson afterwards." Experience is what you get when you are looking for something else. But, the experience of failure always makes you either better of bitter. The choice is up to you. The good news is that God has no plans that end in failure. Jeremiah 29:11 (NIV) says, "For I know the plans I have for you, plans to prosper you and not to harm you, plans to give you hope and a future."

Success consists of getting up just one time more than you fell down. "You don't drown by falling in the water; you drown by staying there," said author Edwin Louis Cole. So get up and go on. Proverbs 28:13 (LB) says, "A man who refuses to admit his mistakes can never be successful, but if he confesses and forsakes them, he gets another chance."

The death of your dream will not be accomplished by a major failure. Its death will come from indifference and apathy. The best way to go on after a failure is to learn the lesson and forget the details. If you don't you'll become like the scalded dog that fears hot water, and afterwards, the cold.

Failure can become a weight or it can give you wings. The only way to make a comeback is to go on. If the truth were known, 99 percent of success is built on former failure. A mistake proves somebody stopped talking long enough to do something.

Never give up on what you know you really should do. The person with big dreams is more powerful than the person with all the facts. Remember, overnight success takes about 10 years. The "man of the hour" spent many days and nights getting there. Consider the man who said, "My overnight success was the longest night of my life." Winners simply do what losers don't want to do.

Earl Nightingale said, "A young man once asked a great and famous older man, 'How can I make a name for myself in the world and become successful?' The great and famous man replied: 'You have only to decide upon what it is you want and then stay with it, never deviating from your course no matter how long it takes, or how rough the road, until you have accomplished it.'" Success is largely a matter of holding on after others have let go.

In the confrontation between the stream and the rock, the stream always wins—not through strength by through perseverance. Christopher Morely said, "Big shots are only little shots that keep shooting." Persistence is simply enjoying the distance between the fulfillment of God's promises.

Judas was an example of someone who started the good fight of faith but lacked persistence. God wants us to be people of strong wills, not strong won'ts. Many of the world's great failures did not realize how close they were to success when they gave up. Stopping at third base adds no more score than striking out. We rate success by what people finish, not by what why start. People do not fail; they just quit too easily. God won't give up on you! Don't you give up on God! "For I am persuaded that neither death, nor life, nor angels, nor principalities, nor powers, nor things present nor things to come, nor height, nor depth, nor any other creature, shall be able to separate us from the love of God, which is in Christ Jesus our Lord" (Romans 8:38-39).

Your persistence is proof you have not yet been defeated. Mike Murdock says, "You have no right to anything you have not pursued. For the proof of desire is the pursuit." So, "Commit to the Lord whatever you do, and your plans will succeed" (Proverbs 16:3, NIV). Life holds no greater wealth than that of steadfast commitment. It cannot be robbed from you. Only you can lose it by your will.

"The destiny of the diligent is to stand in the company of leaders. Seest thou a man diligent in his business? He shall stand before kings" (Proverbs 22:29). When faithfulness is most difficult, it is most necessary; because trying times are no time to quit trying. The secret of success is to start from scratch and keep on scratching. Remember the old poem that says "Success is failure turned inside our, the silver tint of the clouds of doubt, and you never can tell how close you are, it may be near when it seems so far. So stick to the fight when you're hardest hit, it's when things seem worse that you must not quit" (Unknown).

John Mason is the author of eight best-selling books and the founder and president of Insight International.

Marriage & Family

All Charged Up!

Norm Miller

ALL CHARGED UP

by Rob Dilbone

Looking out over the big hole in the backyard that would soon become his new swimming pool, Norm Miller began to question what he was doing. The work was only about half-way completed and he was already thinking of what he would do next. He remembers thinking, "I could tear down that brick wall and put in some French doors." But before he could dream any further, another thought flashed across his mind, "What in the world am I doing? I haven't even had one party here and I'm wanting to change things. I thought this was what life was all about."

Norm Miller was supposed to be happy. He was making good money as a traveling salesman for Interstate(Batteries, a thriving, though relatively young, replacement battery company, but there was always an emptiness inside. He had a beautiful wife, a big house, and nice cars, but still something was missing and he couldn't quite put his finger on it. Then, early one morning while driving home from a party, Norm was pulled over and charged with driving while intoxicated. Not long after, he received his second DWI charge. However, it was not until his third time being pulled over that the light finally went on. Norm talked his way out of a third DWI, but when he woke up the next morning, he realized he deserved to be in jail. He recalls just lying in bed and blurting out, "God, help me! I can't handle it anymore!" It was at that moment that he realized he had become an alcoholic like his father before him.

The Fast Lane

Norm Miller grew up around cars. His dad owned a service station and a four-car garage. He repaired cars, pumped gas and stocked and sold parts. "Almost like an auto parts store today," he recalls. His dad was a good salesman and worked hard. Norm remembers his dad checking the wear and tear of customer's tires while they were getting gas or selling them a new muffler before they took off down the road. His mother was involved in the family business too, and Norm learned very early that if he was going to amount to anything in life he was going to have to work hard. "I guess I was raised with this ethic that you've got to do whatever it takes to get the job done," he says.

His home was not what he would consider today "Christian," although the family did go to Church regularly and prayed at meals. But that was about the extent of their faith and he never remembers the whole experience meaning much to him. His dad was an alcoholic but got "on the wagon" when little Norm was about eight or nine, eventually becoming a deacon in the Church. Although young Norm memorized scriptures and won a few awards, he says, "It all just kind of went in one ear and out the other and I just did my thing and left."

Norm decided as a kid that he was going to have fun in life. He grew up wondering what life was all about and finally decided the purpose of life was to be happy. "The way to be happy," he rationalized, "was to have fun." So as a kid his objectives were to have fun, be happy and party. Galviston was the perfect spot to do all three. In those days the small, port town in southern Texas on the Gulf of Mexico was wide-open. There was gambling and drinking 24 hours a day, open prostitution, and rock-n-roll music to set the tone. Growing up in that atmosphere proved enchanting for Norm and he started drinking by the age of 14. "My whole game plan was to have fun, party and 'kick em up,' that's what my friends and I did and it was easy to do in Galviston."

After graduating from high school, Norm decided to go on to college, but before he left he set several goals. First, he decided he wanted to make a lot of money, which meant he needed to get a decent job after college. Not just any job either, but a good job with money and prestige. Next, he set his sights on a new car. Third, he started searching for a pretty girl to marry. Back in those days many people got married in college and he decided that if he was going to get married, his wife needed to be pretty. Then he wanted a nice house and a car for the wife. Money for parties and travel and two children, one of each, rounded out his list of goals. "I remember thinking all that would surley make me happy," he says with a laugh. Norm not only continued to drink through college, but at one point he actually got into the "booze" business with some enterprising fraternity brothers.

He and his buddies decided to start selling alcohol out of their house. The college campus was located in a "dry" county, so they figured they could make some easy money and have some fun by driving to the next county, buying the beer and liquor, and then selling it to other students for a profit. They formed The High-Low Club and sold memberships for a dollar a piece to raise working capital and then they threw parties for members only and charged everyone for the drinks. Everything was going great until it got too big and became hard work. They decided to close the club down and concentrate on finishing school.

Business & Batteries

After college, Norm returned home to go into business with his dad. His dad, after almost a decade of being sober, had started drinking again, though not nearly as much as before. Norm's father soon sold the service station and asked Norm to move to Memphis and go into business with him as distributors with Interstate Batteries. Norm did and business was pretty good, but after a couple years Norm decided to take the opportunity to move back to Texas and work for Interstate's founder, Mr. John Sursey. Norm traveled around the country selling batteries and opening franchises. His drinking and partying continued as the business grew, but he tried not to let it interfere with his business.

Like Norm had planned, he found his wife-to-be at college. Anne, it turned out, had also been raised in Galviston, but because she was four years younger, they had never met in school. In the summer of 1962 they got engaged, but three months before the wedding Norm was "called up" for active duty with the Air Force Reserve due to the Cuban missile crisis. Their plans were put on hold until the crisis ended. Finally, they were married on December 29, 1962. Married life was good in the beginning, but by the time they moved back to Texas, Anne had grown tired of Norm's drinking and partying and decided that one day she would leave him, she simply had to wait for the right time.

Norm worked hard at Interstate and the company continued to grow at a steady clip. Unfortunately, so did his thirst for alcohol. By the time he was stopped for his third DWI, he had been blacking out once a week on average from too much alcohol. After his backyard philosophical revelation and subsequent DWIs, he decided to try Alcoholics Anonymous. "I went to AA meetings for about six or eight weeks, but I didn't even read the book," he recalls.

About this same time a friend happened to start mentioning the Bible. He told Norm the Bible was the Word of God and in it were many truths by which he could live his life. "I told him to prove it to me," he recalls. "If you can prove it is the Word of God, I'll pay attention, but as far as I'm concerned it's an old book written by a bunch of old dudes from long ago and I don't need it." Over time the friend supplied Norm with enough information to convince him of the Bible's validity. He remembers that three areas nailed it down for him: archeology, methodology and fulfilled prophecy. "I started reading the Bible and going to a Bible study. I came across the scripture in Galatians 5:22 where it talks about the fruit of the Spirit being peace, love and joy. I remember saying, 'That's what I want.'" Eventually, Norm prayed and received his salvation at a Bible study one night and he has never looked back.

What's the Norm

Today, home is just Norm and Anne. They have two grown children, who both live only about five minutes away, and five grand children. Both Anne and Norm are very involved in a variety of different ministries. About three years ago, Anne started a mission in Dallas called Women of Vision. Norm is active in, among many others, a prison ministry. He also keeps busy with the business of Interstate and racing. While evangelism is his passion, racing is certainly more than just his hobby.

In 1991, Joe Gibbs, the former coach of the NFL champion Washington Redskins, approached Norm about sponsoring his car on the NASCAR circuit. The two have been racing together ever since. Their team won the Daytona 500 in 1993 and the relationship has been a win/win for Gibbs, Interstate and Norm. The two men have found common ground not only in their enthusiasm for racing, but in their faith as well. Gibbs says, "Norm shares his personal relationship with the Lord with his employees and others who come in contact with him. It is evident to everyone that Norm is honest and fair with his employees and business associates."

Norm is now Chairman of Interstate and his brother Tommy is President. He doesn't spend as much time in the office on a day to day basis as he used to, but he is still very involved in the planning and direction of the company. Norm Miller is probably best described as a racing-businessman-evangelist. When he stepped down as president at the age of 52, he remembers thinking. "What am I going to do with the rest of my life?" He also realized, as he recalls, "One day I am going to stand before God and have to give an account from now until then. I could say I sold more batteries than anyone and He would say, 'Well, so what?' I want to be part of millions coming to Christ. That's my prayer. That's where I have put my efforts and time."

I guess you could say Norm Miller is "Charged up and off to the races!"

OVERCOMING BEING *OVERLY* COMMITTED

by Larry Burkett

In turning away from struggling to meet the world's standard of success, we can salvage the most important thing in our lives— our families.

I have never been in bondage to debt, even as a non-Christian. I simply hate paying interest to anyone, so even if I borrowed money in business I always paid it back as quickly as possible. However, I have experienced business bondage of a different sort.

When I was in college, I was working 10 to 14 hour days at Cape Canaveral, Florida, and carrying a full load in school as well. It took me nearly six years to finish. I then went into a variety of businesses, simply substituting the hours in school for hours at work.

I actually believed this was the normal pattern for success, because it was the pattern of most of the successful business people I knew. What I did not realize then was that most of them were working on their second or third marriages and were repeating the same pattern that had wrecked the previous relationships.

Eventually, I found the Lord as my Savior and real-ized my priorities were out of balance. I began taking Sundays off to attend church, but within a few months I started falling back into the same old routine. With each new challenge came the need for more time.

You Can't Say it Clearer Than That

One morning I came home about 2 a.m. and crawled into bed, only to wake up a few minutes later with a Scripture verse vividly implanted in my mind. At the time, I did not even know they made concordances, so I spent the better part of two hours searching through my Bible. Finally, I found the verse I was looking for: "It is vain for you to rise up early, to retire late, to eat the bread of painful labors; for He gives to His beloved even in his sleep." (Psalm 127:2 NASB).

You can't say it clearer than that. When I became a Christian, I promised God He would never have to deal with my disobedience if only He would make His will for my life so clear I could not misunderstand it. Psalm 127:2 did that for me. From that point on I made a commit-ment to never again spend endless hours pursuing suc-cess. I limited myself to a maximum 48-hour workweek and have maintained that schedule ever since. I find that I can accomplish more and make better use of my time than when I worked twice as many hours. I also won't have to look back at age 65 or 70 and say, "I wish I had done that 20 years ago."

How sad it would be to face death and realize you'd missed God's best for your life. At that point, it does not matter if you're successful materially or even if you gave large sums of money to God's work.

It seems to me that the preponderance of Scripture teaches that God wants us to shine like a candle in the darkness, not fizzle out as a Roman candle. A frazzled, frustrated Christian whose focus is always on material success is like a bolt of lightning: one bright flash, then darkness again.

If you find you can't keep your time in the right balance, I suggest a plan that a friend shared with me several years ago. Just ask God to either give you the wisdom to maintain the correct priorities or the courage to shut down the business!

Perhaps the worst offender I ever knew, when it came to working too much, was not a businessperson but a pastor. His story illustrates the terrible consequences of having our priorities out of order.

It's Never Too Late

Evan was the pastor of a large evangelical church and spent almost every waking moment there. Even when he was at home, his mind was at his office. Although his family was having problems, he prided himself on never allowing those problems to interfere with his ministry activities.

Then one Sunday morning the local police chief called. The pastor's 16-year-old son had been arrested for drug possession, again. The previous day his wife had suffered an emotional breakdown and had been committed to the psychiatric ward at a local hospital. As Evan hung up the phone that Sunday morning, he realized his whole life was a lie. He was in bondage to his own ego and pride. He would have counseled any businessperson in the same situation to drop the business and get his or her life straightened out.

That Sunday morning, he stood in the pulpit and told his congregation, my life is a wreck and I'm a phony. My wife is in a mental ward, my son is in jail for using drugs, and I don't know if God still wants me in the ministry. So as of this minute I am resigning as your pastor. I'm going to try to salvage my relationship with God and my family. If I'm successful, I'll be back—if you still want me. Otherwise I will assume God has other plans for my life."

Evan was gone for several months, during which time the church used interim pastors and guest speakers. He spent that time ministering to his wife and working with his son in the detention home.

When he returned, things were much different. The biggest change in the church was that Evan required the deacons to become leaders and relieve him of the responsibility of doing all the counseling, development and planning. He had learned what many other Christians never learn until it's too late: God does not need us to burn out for Him. He would much rather have us wear out gracefully. In discovering this simple truth, Evan was able to salvage his marriage, his relationship with his son, and his relationship with God.

True Success

We are servants of the living God, and when our "success" binds us, we cannot fulfill our function. That function includes walking in a manner worthy of the Lord, pleasing Him in all respects, bearing fruit in every good work, and increasing in the knowledge of God (Colossians 1:10).

Many Christians who are overly committed to work try to rationalize it by saying, "It's for my family." A simple way to test this rationalization is to put it to a vote. Most wives and children would vote for more time with Dad, not money.

Being overly committed in business is usually due to a lack of faith, which results in fear especifically, the fear of failure. But if we really believe God is in control, we also should believe that He is able to make us "truly" successful while we are keeping our lives in balance.

"How blessed is the man who finds wisdom, and the man who gains understanding. For its profit is better than the profit of silver, and its gain than fine gold" (Proverbs 3:13-14).

Larry Burkett is a best-selling author, speaker, and financial counselor. He is founder and president of Christian Financial Concepts, Inc. in Gainesville, GA. Money Matters, his radio call-in program, is heard by thousands of Americans each day across America.

UNLIMITED GROWTH UNPARALLELED DISASTER

by Daryl Kraft

Success beyond measure is one option. Complete disaster the other. The deciding factor is your attention to detail

I was totally unprepared for what occurred one spring morning as I was getting dressed for work. I was complaining—as usual—to my wife Sherryl that my shirt wasn't perfectly starched. As I glanced out the window into the back yard, I noticed the dogs' wear and tear in one of the flower beds, so I mentioned that to her as well. Then I went on to quiz her about money she had spent on a shower gift for a friend. In other words, it was a typical morning for me.

Finally, as I was standing with my briefcase in hand, ready to leave for work, waiting for my usual good-bye kiss, Sherryl began to cry. As I watched, dumbfounded, not knowing what was wrong or what to do, her body began convulsing with sobs as she tried to stifle her sorrow and hide her tears behind her hands. I moved to her side, horrified at her anguish.

"Sherryl," I finally asked softly, "what in the world is wrong?"

189

Barely able to speak, she sobbed, "I just can't take it anymore."

I saw how broken and sincere she was, so after a few moments I asked, "What can't you take anymore?"

She looked at me with a countenance that reflected just how emotionally shattered she really was. Apparently my previous response over being home for dinner gave her the courage to finally share what had been tearing her apart for years. "I can't stand your continual criticism of me. I've tried as hard as I know how for the past 12 years to please you, but I just can't make you happy."

Self-Justification Works Wonders

Though I was shaken by her tears and emotion, at first I wondered, "Have I really been that critical?" Sure, I might have come down a bit hard when requiring that our house be neat and orderly. And maybe I had been a little too fussy about the yard and my clothes. But then, as Sherryl's tears and words hit home, I began to hear myself asking why my shirt hadn't been ironed just right; why my favorite meal had not been prepared like I wanted it; why she let the kids get away with so much; how and why she spent money; and on, and on, and on.

"Still," I rationalized to myself, "didn't she know I thought everything was 99 percent good? Didn't she realize how much I appreciated her? Didn't I give her everything she wanted? Wasn't my nit-picking insignificant compared to the good things I was doing for her and our family?"

This time my usual process of self-justification was stopped dead in its tracks as she continued, "I just wish

I could die so you can marry someone else who will make you happy."

Her words literally shook my world. In total shock I dropped my briefcase and began to silently take stock of our marriage. I vividly remembered the day on campus of Biola University when I first saw the woman I knew I wanted as my wife. I was walking to class when the most beautiful girl I had ever seen stepped out of the library and paused under an olive tree to talk to several of her friends.

Much later—after dating, courtship, and years of marriage—I found out that life for Sherryl had not been so beautiful. But because I was too immature to understand, for years I saw only the things I wanted to see—her servant's heart, her generosity, her selfless caring for the children and me. I wasn't aware that she longed to simply have a warm, loving home. Not a huge, fancy house—but just a home of her own where she felt loved.

Now she literally wished she was dead. Why? So her husband could be "happier." How could I have brought her to this point of loneliness and desperation? Where had I missed the mark in our marriage? Worse yet, why didn't she know I loved her?

"Haven't I told you I love you?" I asked.

"Only when we were intimate," she said. "That tells me that you love me only for sex instead of loving me for myself."

Instead of exploding with defensiveness like I might have done before, I was taken back to that day I held my heart up to God and asked Him to take over. He was obviously answering my prayer, because now I found myself listening in quiet shame and embarrassment. God was in the process of giving me the freedom of wanting to listen to Sherryl and to take to heart whatever she was willing to share. I put my arms around her and asked, "Why didn't you say something sooner?"

"I thought you would just get mad at me," she softly replied.

As we stood there holding each other, tears filling our eyes, neither of us could speak. Finally, realizing for the first time the enormity of what I had been doing to my wife, I prayed in desperation, "Lord, help me to change. Help me not to incessantly criticize my wife anymore. God, I don't want to have a critical spirit toward the person I say I love the most. Forgive me for nearly destroying an already broken person. Lord, because You know my heart, You can help me to understand, to become someone who heals rather than hurts my wife. Beginning today, Lord, I don't want to criticize her or anyone else ever again."

In the days following that prayer, I began to notice more and more injunctions in God's Word against a spirit of criticism and words that hurt rather than heal. For instance:

"...put...aside...abusive speech..." (Colossians 3:8).

"Let no unwholesome word proceed from your mouth, but only such a word as is good for edification" (Ephesians 4:29).

"Let him who means to love life and see good days refrain his tongue...from speaking guile" (1 Peter 3:10).

As the Lord continued working on my heart with these verses and others, a troubling question arose in my mind: how could I have always considered murder and adultery as sins I would never commit, yet have been so free with critical comments and condemning attitudes? Was it because I did not believe a critical spirit was as bad a sin before God? Was it because there's no social or political law against it? Or was it because I didn't believe criticism and condemning words hurt others as much as murder or adultery?

Through this, God opened my eyes to a whole new perspective on the horrible sin of a critical spirit and critical words with everyone else in all my relationships.

"...the tongue is a small thing, but what enormous damage it can do. A great forest [marriage] can be set on fire by one tiny spark [teasing, nit-picking, criticism, constant disapproval]. And the tongue is a flame of fire. It is full of wickedness and poisons every part of the body. And the tongue is set on fire by hell itself, and can turn our whole lives into a blazing flame of destruction [of our mate and kids] and disaster." James 3:5-6 (TLB)

I realized that if this was true, it meant that my criticism was destroying—literally killing—my wife! No wonder my many years of criticism and nagging had worn Sherryl down to a point of utter desperation.

From that point on, I prayed that criticism, nit-picking, a critical spirit, and all my harsh words of disapproval would not only entirely disappear from my conversation, but from my attitudes as well.

Recently I was talking with one of our franchisees—also a competitive athlete—and telling him how God was helping me see the kind of trauma even one critical word can inflict on my wife. In order to drive home the gravity of a husband's criticism, I asked him to imagine what it would be like if I doubled up my fist and hit my wife full-force in the face (which, of course, I would never do). Though I might apologize, my apology wouldn't heal her broken jaw. And though she would forgive me, it would take weeks, even months, for the pain to go away and the injury to heal.

This is a vivid illustration of the kind of enormous damage our words can inflict on our wives and others. Now I understand that those little critical words I used to consider "no big deal" were actually "full of wickedness and poisons," with the potential to bring long-lasting, continuous pain to my wife, or even to ultimately destroy our marriage.

My #1 Customer

One day, as I was reading I Peter, God began to show me that not only should I seek to never criticize my wife, but also that she should be my number one "customer." In other words, as I go about my professional life in addition to my personal life, I should never put any customer or client before my spouse.

I Peter 3:7 says, "You husbands likewise, live with your wives in an understanding way, as with a weaker vessel, since she is a woman; and grant her honor as a fellow-heir of the grace of life, so that your prayers may not be hindered."

Even though I was more regularly coming home for dinner on time, I had been ready to jump at a moment's notice to keep my business customers happy—at the same time expecting the one "client" I professed to love the most to be satisfied with whatever time was left over. My business customer got "prime time," while my wife got very little time. And often even when I was with her I continued to be preoccupied with my "real" customers.

In essence, God was saying, "Daryl, don't bother praying to me about your business or anything else if you're not sensitive toward and considerate of Sherryl's needs. I won't even hear you!"

Gradually I began to understand that God's priority for me was that I should live with Sherryl—not my business customers—in a way that showed continual sensitivity, understanding and consideration for her above and before all others.

Success beyond measure is available for those who choose it—and who are willing to pay the small price to gain it.

Daryl Kraft is the president and founder of Environment Control Building Maintenance Company with 65 franchises in 23 States. Excerpted with permission of Bridge-Logos Publishers, North Brunswick, NJ. Copyright 1997, from The Businessman's Guide to Real Success by Daryl Kraft.

6 Basics of being a Great Dad

by Bob Hamrin, Ph.D.

Finding the ultimate investment
into your family's future.

There are a couple of fatherhood fundamentals we
should all be aware of. One is what God expects of
each father. The other is what each child wants from his
or her dad.

The big picture on fathering is given in the final verse
of the Old Testament. Malachi 4:6 says, "He will turn the
hearts of fathers to their children, and the hearts of the
children to their fathers; or else I will come and strike the
land with a curse." God clearly desires that father's hearts
be turned to their children.

The good news is that fathers have the ability to
influence their child's life in the most fundamental way.
The children make this clear. Teens were asked what
most shaped their self-image. Two powerful factors were
(1) A close relationship with father (2) spending a lot of
time with father. This is father power—exercised in a
positive way.

The bad news is that many dads are exercising
negative father power. One of the most tragic facts of

contemporary American society is pervasive Father Absence. Over 36 percent of children—24.7 million—do not have their biological father physically present in their home. Of the 64% of dads who are physically present, at least 25 percent are emotionally absent from their children. That's another 10.8 million children. These two statistics total to a startling fact, over half of America's children—around 35.5 million—suffer from Father Absence on a daily basis.

Thousands of teens were asked what single question they would like their parents to answer, 50% said "Do you love me?" And when teens under stress were asked where they turn to for help in a crisis, dads ranked 48th on the list!

Every dad is faced with some basic choices. Do I invest my main energies in my work or leisure time, and leave the nurturing to mom (or to no one), or do I invest myself in my children, giving them the unconditional love and nurturing they need and deserve?

The potential is there, the father must choose which it will be. To achieve this potential, the following 6 Basics of Being a Great Dad will help. These basics come from the Bible and from kids' hearts. Here are the 6 Basics:

1.   Provide unconditional love and affection. Unconditional love is love of a very special kind. It means loving your child for the unique, infinitely valuable person that he or she is, regardless of performance, attitude, behavioral pattern or specific behavior. For dads who wonder, "But how can I show my kids unconditional love?" There are four key ways: First, see the uniqueness of each child of God; Second, build them up; Third, discipline them well; And fourth, give them your blessing.

2.   Spend T-I-M-E. Children spell love T-I-M-E. For most dads, this is the greatest challenge, and the facts bear this out. Two documented surveys of dads' actual one-on-one time with their children found the cumulative time together in a day to be 37 seconds and 35 seconds respectively. Clearly, the major challenge for most dads is to find a healthy work/family balance. The key is this: Follow your heart. Make those three words your standard operating procedure, and you won't go wrong!

3.   Communicate constantly and creatively. Despite the fact that dads ranked 48th on the list of where teens turn under stress, there is good news: teens do want to talk to their parents. So what are the ABCs of good communication? First, listen, and listen actively, which means listening to feelings. Second, ask. Be interested in their world. Ask them how you are doing as a dad. Third, share. Share about your job, your successes and your failures.

4.   Partner with mom. Another vital principle is that God wants you and your wife to be one master. Matthew 6:24 says, "No one can serve two masters." Put this great truth into practice and you'll make life much simpler and better for your children. Remember that one of the two things that kids say they most want is for "their parents to stay together." This old adage is true: one of the greatest things a dad can do for his kids is to love mom. It is really quite simple for dads who are married: stay married and love your wife. Do whatever it takes to build, or rebuild, a healthy and vibrant marriage. It's never too tough or too late. For dads who are no longer married, partner with your former spouse by keeping the interests of the children first and foremost, try to see them as often as possible, and stay in touch constantly.

5.   Instill moral and spiritual values. One of the main cries of adolescents today is for their need for their parents to give them a moral and spiritual value system. According to Robert Coles, a Christian psychologist at Harvard, this involves giving your children a strong set of values, which will give them a better chance in life. The key question for each dad to ask himself is: "What am I doing about my child's spiritual development?" All too many dads draw a big zero in this area when it should be one of our highest priorities as a dad.

6.   Establish a fathering legacy. The tragic irony here is that not too many fathers have given this much explicit attention, yet it is one of the most important matters a father could ever deal with. This isn't about money, houses, cars, etc. We are talking about the values, principles and virtues that a dad will instill in his children that are going to guide them through all of life's challenges and difficult periods. These values will be so deeply instilled that they will be passed on to their children, down through the generations. Through his fathering legacy, a man can leave a mark on this world that far exceeds his fondest hopes and dreams. Each dad should examine his work and ask: "What long-term and significant impact will that have?"

Good news or bad news

The bad news is that following these 6 Basics of being a great dad is tough. Many personal, social, and vocational forces constantly pull us away from the great dad pathway.

Yet the good news is that any father can be a great dad—if he truly turns his heart to each child, and makes a lifelong commitment to them. The incredibly good news is that he will experience one of the deepest and richest sources of joy—the joy of fathering.

Dr. Robert Hamrin is the founder and president of Great Dads. This national ministry provides "The 6 Basics of Being a Great Dad" seminar to companies and churches. To find out about hosting a seminar, call 1-888-GRTDADS and visit their website at www.greatdads.org

COMPOUNDING FAMILY INTEREST

by Steve Farrar

The capital you are investing into your family today is guaranteed to bring a return—even 100 years from now

How do you affect your family in a positive way for the next 100 years? By doing something today. By being obedient today. And then by doing something tomorrow. And one day those small deposits will begin to add up. Every time you love your wife as Christ loved the church, every time you live with your wife in an understanding way, every time you grant your wife honor as fellow heir of the grace of life, you are putting away principal. It's like money in the bank.

Every time you take the time to listen to one of your kids, every time you bow your head and ask God to lead you and your family for that day, every time you refuse to alter your expense account to pick up a few extra bucks, every time you pray for a guy who stabbed you in the back in order to get a job promotion that should have gone to you, God sees those actions. And He will reward those actions.

In other words, every time you obey Christ and His word, it's as though you are making a deposit of spiritual capital. And every time you obey the Lord, He immediately matches your spiritual contribution of obedience.

One day you'll look around and begin to see that your children are picking up momentum spiritually that they will pass on to their children. And it's quite probable that your compound interest will begin to pick up steam right about the time you reach the end of your earthly life. Just as you are ready to check out, the compounding effect will begin to pick up momentum beyond your wildest dreams.

This is estate planning at its finest. And when you leave this kind of spiritual inheritance to your children, it's all tax free.

Watching the Interest Grow

Crawford and I have been friends for nearly 15 years. He is a gifted communicator who walks the talk (perhaps you've had the privilege of hearing Crawford speak at Promise Keepers).

Every time I'm with Crawford, I think "compound interest." In Crawford's study, he has on his wall a family tree that was handwritten by his grandfather, Milton. It's quite a document. It begins with a man by the name of Peter Loritts. Peter was a slave who gained his freedom at the end of the Civil War.

About one hundred and thirty years ago, Crawford's great-grandfather, Peter, established a small town not too far from what is now the Charlotte Motor Speedway. Peter had worked very, very hard all of his life and had somehow managed to scrape together a few hundred dollars. With that money, Peter was able to buy some acreage. The land that Peter bought eventually became the town of Conover, North Carolina. A number of former slaves and their families comprised the town of Conover. Peter donated some land so that they could build their own church and have their own cemetery.

Peter could neither read or write, but he knew the Bible from the sermons and stories that he had heard. Because he loved the Savior of the Bible, he obeyed the Bible to the best of his ability.

Peter married a godly woman and was blessed with three children, a daughter and two sons, one named Milton who wrote out the family tree. Milton and his wife had seven boys and seven girls. The youngest boy was Crawford's father. Crawford's dad went home to be with the Lord a few years ago at the age of eighty one.

Old Peter taught his children to love and follow Jesus Christ and showed them what it was to be a man. They saw him work hard, love their mother and love them. Peter not only led his family, but he was always quick to help another family who had a financial need. His children saw his example. Peter's son's grew up and worked hard, loved their wives and loved their children. Why? Because God was at the center of their homes.

Then the next generation came along, and once again, Jesus Christ was at the center of their lives. The boys of that generation became godly men and the girls became godly women. Crawford's dad told him that, as a young boy, he would watch his grandfather Peter, the former slave, in his eighties, sitting on his rocker on the porch, passing each day singing praises to the Lord and telling his grandchildren about the greatness of Jesus.

God is still accruing his compound interest on Crawford's family. In the Loritts family there is a strong tradition of male leadership. There is a strong tradition of husbands loving their wives and children, and a tradition that husbands do not walk out on their families. There is a strong tradition of Jesus Christ being at the center of each day's responsibilities. My friend, Crawford, is the fourth generation from the old slave, Peter. Every time Crawford looks at the family tree, and every time Crawford looks in the mirror, he sees compound interest.

God is already blessing the fifth generation with the compound interest that God has accrued to Old Peter's account. When you meet Crawford's children, you see the goodness of God to the fifth generation. One of Crawford's sons has just enrolled in seminary to prepare for a lifetime of service to the same Lord that saved his great, great, grandfather.

So how do you lead your family for the next 100 years? You do it the same way that Peter Loritts did it. You do it by being a godly father today, and then you do it again tomorrow. Putting away spiritual capital is living in obedience to Christ doing the stuff today that most men are too preoccupied to do. That's what old Peter did in North Carolina. He did what he needed to do each day to be a disciple of Jesus. That's the job of a Christian father. Not to be wildly successful or not to be well-known—just to be faithful. God sees His faithful men, and rewards His faithful men.

Steve Farrar is the founder and Chairman of Men's Leadership Ministries with offices in Bryan, Texas. Each year he speaks to thousands of men, equipping them to be more effective spiritual leaders in their homes. He is the author of Standing Tall, How a Man Can Protect His Family, the best-selling Point Man and the new Anchor Man, from which this article was excerpted with permission (Thomas Nelson Publishers, 1998). Steve and his wife Mary live with their three children near Dallas, Texas.

10 Practical Ideas to Build a Thriving Marriage

by Patrick Morley

The truth is, even the best marriage could be better

Can you remember how your heart pounded the first time you knew you loved your mate? Whatever happened to those feelings? A good marriage should be like great music—passionate, harmonious, and colorful. But did you know that today nearly 40% of Christian marriages end in divorce? What can we do about that?

We each marry for the same reasons. We dream of building a life, together, meteoric career success, and doting children—to spend the rest of our life with that person who knocked us off our feet! Yet, under the weight of a thousand daily pressures those dreams often fade away. In this article I would like to share with you the ten most practical ideas I know of to help grow that loving feeling—to make beautiful music with the mate you love.

If you can, read this together with your mate out loud. By the way, if you are single, engaged, or divorced you can still read these ten ideas with great benefit. So without further adieu...

1. Listen to Each other. Communication invariably shows up as the number one problem in marriage surveys. The greatest weakness in communication with our mates is the problem of giving an overly quick reply. We attach high value to our mates when we listen deeply to each other without giving any overly quick response that criticizes or gives advice (two things all people dread). Listening lubricates marriage and keeps down friction.

2. Spend Time Together Alone. The issue is time—who gets it? How we spend our time reveals what is really important to us. Successful couples spend time together. They read the Bible together. They develop shared interests, like bowling, reading, hiking, or plays.

3. Touch Each Other. Successful couples touch each other. They hug, squeeze, embrace, pat, hold hands, put arms around each other, and sit close enough to touch when sitting in front of the tube. Non-sexual touching leads to genuine intimacy. They enjoy sex, and often.

4. Encourage Each Other With Words. Encouragement is the food of the heart, and every heart is a hungry heart. Our mate has an emotional bank account into which we make deposits and from which we make withdrawals—like being grumpy when we get home from work or encouraging our spouse when they feel down. We all need to be lifted up when we are blue, but the most successful couples go another step. Successful couples create a positive environment. They verbally affirm each other at every opportunity. They try to catch each other doing things "right." They pass along compliments others make about their mate. They never pass up an opportunity to express appreciation. "I love

the way you fix your hair." "That was a great dinner." "Thank you for being such a good provider."

5. Unconditionally Accept Each Other. A man under stress said, "The reason I love my dog so much is because he love me no matter what I do." Unconditional love and acceptance forms a crucial foundation in successful marriages. The most intense need of every man and woman is to be in relationship with one other person who really cares. Happy couples do not feel like they have to perform to be loved. They do not feel like they will be rejected if they do not meet a set of standards. Intimacy means that I know who you are at the deepest level, and I accept you. Jesus accepts us, "Just as I am," and smart mates accept each other as is, too.

6. Be Committed to Each Other. Successful couples have a commitment to work through troubles. The "divorce" word is not allowed to be uttered, no matter how upset or angry one becomes. They have an agreement on how to handle conflicts. They have talked through issues of how to "fight fair" under peaceful conditions. They try to let the little ones go. They make an active commitment to want the best for their mate, to help them grow as a person. Be sure to pray for both "for" and "with" each other—you may be the only person in the whole world regularly praying for your mate.

7. Take Care of Your Financial Future Together. Money problems create more stress on marriage than any other outside threat. Here is the issue: is it right to spend so much on a lifestyle today that your mate will be forced to abandon it when you are gone? Successful couples have resolved to live within their means. They do not live so high today that they fail to provide for retirement and premature death. They do not take on

debt. They know that Morley's Money Maxim is true: "Debt is dumb."

8. Laugh With Each Other. The antidote for boredom in marriage is lively humor. If your partner tell a funny, laugh! (Even if he is not Bob Hope or she is not Carol Burnett). If neither one of you is funny, make sure to watch funny movies and be around funny friends.

9. Make Each Other Your Top Priority. Once I called three friends to pray for a difficult challenge I faced the next day. One week later I finally called each of them to let them know how it turned out. I am sure I have shown the same disinterest to my friends. The only one you can fully count on to be there for you is your mate. The rule of rules for successful marriage is this: After God, but before all others, make each other your top priority. Do not let anyone—not even your children, but especially your parents—come between you.

10. Be Each Other's Best Friend. Oswald Chambers said, "The last mark of intimacy is to share our secret joys." Happy couples commit to spend time together as friends. They share secrets with each other. They enjoy each other's company. They realize they are the only ones who are really in this thing "together." Everyone else is for themselves to some degree, even kids. But couples are "one flesh."

The
Bottom Line

Daryl Kraft

THE BOTTOM LINE

When you have all you need, and still want more, you
know it's time to change the bottom line

by Brian Mast

Business was expanding and proving very profitable
for Daryl Kraft. After only 10 short years since graduating
from college, his small business in southern California had
grown to the point of needing to create a chain of
franchises to meet the rising demands. From the outside,
Daryl seemed to have it all.

At the personal level, however, Daryl Kraft was stressed
out. He was taking up to six Valium a day, he says, "just to
cope with the anxiety, criticisms, and people-
disappointments associated with my success." His marriage
to his college sweetheart was already on the rocks and life
at home was anything but peaceful. Something needed
to change, but Daryl didn't know what to do or where to
start.

It was then he received word that his close cousin,
Dave, who had been battling a terminal illness, had only a
few more weeks left to live. Several days later, as Daryl stood
at Dave's bedside, he began to see what was so
desperately missing in his own life. Dave, who had wasted
away to a mere 90 pounds, was still full of joy and peace
as he said good-bye to his young wife and two kids, ages 3
and 5. "Standing at the foot of his bed," Daryl remembers,
"I could see that he had a peace dying that I didn't have
living. Even more amazing was that he had everything I

wanted without having any of the things I had." The 5,500 square foot home, the cars, the hunting trips to Alaska and the money in the bank, none of it gave Daryl peace, which was the one possession he really wanted.

Enough is enough!

Daryl left his cousin's bedside a changed man. The peace that Dave exhibited was enough to challenge anyone, but what shook Daryl the most was the understanding of why he didn't have that same peace. "As I stood at the foot of my cousin's bed," Daryl explains, "I realized that he knew the Lord in a way that I didn't."

That revelation shook Daryl to his foundations. He had grown up the son of a minister, he had attended a Christian college, he was the chairman of the elder board and pulpit committee, and he had been teaching an adult Sunday school class for ten years. These accomplishments, however, did nothing to fill the drive for more in his life. "The striking reality," Daryl says,"was that God's peace comes from knowing Him—not from doing things for Him."

He returned home with a burning passion just to know God. He started reading Proverbs, all the while, he says, "crying out in my spirit to know God in a way I never had before." The only other times that Daryl had ever felt the same driving passion was when he was trying to hunt down a record size Kodiak bear in Alaska or trying to become a winning racket ball player. Daryl pleaded, "God, I will trade everything I have—take my title of President, my trophy Kodiak bear (which is mounted and sitting life-size in his living room), take the money I have in my bank account and my two-karat diamond ring—I trade it all to know you the way my cousin Dave knows you."

When Daryl uttered these words, he explains, "That was the beginning of life for me." His life began to be transformed as God revealed things to him through the Scriptures he had never understood before. Suddenly, he admits, "God's word began to come alive, exposing and convicting me of things I would have previously denied, like loving success and using my wife, plus being critical and nit-picking of her." For 12 painful years he and Sherryl had put up with each other, and since neither of them believed in divorce, their future was worse than bleak. They had even reached a point where talking without arguing was not a possibility.

His business, he came to realize, "was the crucible in which God exposed many things I didn't realize about myself." As Daryl confessed his wrongdoings, he felt as if God were "slowly replacing parts of my old nature heart with His heart." As a result, his relationship with his wife began to change. "Today," he says with a mixture of humility and pride, "my wife and I are best friends—praise God!"

The change in his marriage and family didn't come quickly or easily, but as it did, he began to wonder if he should get out of business and into some form of "ministry." Daryl's dad gave him this advice: "Son, don't get out of anything. Make a decision to start living for the Lord where you are and if God wants to move you, He will move you."

But what does it really mean to live for the Lord where you work? Daryl pondered the question as he searched God's Word for answers. In prior years, he assumed being a "Christian boss" meant offering a Monday morning Bible study, tithing off his income, and sharing his testimony with employees.

Today, Daryl says his primary desire is to know how the Lord would think, feel and act in every circumstance of each day. "I used to believe God saved me to save others," he explains, "but now I believe God saved me to change me—and then draw others to Himself through the fruit of

215

that change." The effects of truth, love, respect, humility and integrity have had the expected result: business has continued to boom.

More than Enough

Environment Control Building Maintenance Company has come a long way in the last 36 years. While at college, Daryl and his wife were asked by a graduating friend to take over a few accounts. They took the job and began cleaning commercial office buildings at night. Not only did it pay the bills, but they soon had over 25 customers and needed to hire several other student friends to meet the demand.

After graduation, Daryl's friends called and asked him if he would be interested in helping get them set up with a similar business in their area. Five working partnerships were created in the mid to late '60s. By 1970, business had grown to the point of needing to expand through a franchising program. A corporation was formed, and without any promotion, word quickly spread about the franchise opportunities among the families and friends of the five original franchises. In fact, there has never been a marketing campaign to sell the franchises, but today there are 65 companies operating in 23 states with a consolidated billing of 30 million a year.

Coeur d'Alene, Idaho, now the headquarters for Environment Control (EC), is where a full-time staff of 32 employees provides complete support services to these companies. They not only do all the bookkeeping for each franchise, including payrolls, invoicing, P & L's, tax deposits, reporting, etc., but they also provide a legal support and insurance department that buys all the required group insurances. In addition, they have a department that develops training and sales videos and materials exclusively for EC franchises. This department also works directly with each company to provide direction on growth, profitability and organizational development.

Why take such efforts to help each franchise become established? The answer is summarized in the corporation's purpose statement, "EC... It's about lives." The deep level of commitment affects everyone, from the franchise owners and customers to the employees and vendors. "The fact is, we believe there is only one right way to do business," Daryl states, "and that is to keep the best interest of others our top priority." Environment Contol's committment to others is evidenced at all levels of the business. For example, one third of all managing owners earn six figure incomes and many new franchises have been purchased by existing franchisees.

However, the greatest example of Environment Control's commitment to lives is the royalty arrangement. "Our royalty is a participation in the profits of every company," Daryl points out. "Every other franchise business in the world that I'm aware of takes their royalty off the sales, while ours is a percentage of the bottom line." That simply means that if a franchise is not profitable using the EC program, as Daryl points out, "then EC should not profit either."

Daryl is in the business for the "long haul," and notes that it usually takes about nine months for a company that starts from scratch to turn a profit. If the franchise doesn't make a profit, for whatever the reason, it affects everyone. In that case, Daryl points out, "Not only do we have an unhappy manager, but the startup has taken a toll on a family that has made a sacrifice to get involved in their own business." Each franchise is therefore a huge investment in time and corporate energy, but as Daryl explains, "We are committed to the best interest of these companies for life.

For Daryl Kraft, many things have changed, especially his bottom line. Today, his family is in order, his wife is his best friend and he knows that trusting God is more important than doing things for God. He would not trade the peace and joy he has today for anything. After all, nothing would ever satisfy anyway.

THE PAIN OF DIPLOMACY

by Robert Wolgemuth

Don't let anybody fool you: It is what you say and how you say it!

I come from a long line of accomplished diplomats. These men—many of them ministers—knew the art of carefully crafting their presentations so as not to appear critical or judgmental. In business parlance, these folks were brilliant salespeople.

When I was conceived, a dump truck loaded with these diplomacy genes backed up and emptied itself onto my little developing embryo. Most children say "Da Da" or "Bwanky" first. My opening words were, "Okay, but would you consider option number three?"

These skills helped me to be a good salesman, but they really got in the way at home. "What are you trying to say?" My wife used to blanch when she thought I was trying to "sell" her something. "Why are you acting that way, Daddy?" my kids would ask when I attempted to "communicate" in subtle, non-verbal ways. Diplomacy in the wrong setting started looking a lot like manipulation and my family didn't appreciate it.

After a while, I learned that absolute candor, spoken in tender words, was the most loving thing I could bring to my family. Sure, choosing an appropriate setting and time was still important, but my wife and my children didn't want me to beat around the bush. They wanted to know what I was thinking . . . so I told them. And they appreciated it. This took some practice and some courage, but soon it felt natural. My family liked the new me.

If my brand of diplomacy doesn't work at home, maybe I should try the same kind of candor during the day. I had to put this idea to the test within a few weeks.

Our company was in the process of downsizing. We had grown too quickly and foolishly added too many people. I had to let some people go.

My diplomacy genes kicked in. Be gentle, they called to me. Let these people down easy, they shouted from every cell in my body. My family had taught me that sometimes diplomacy is more painful than candor. My granddaddy used to say, "Nothing is more dangerous than a dull knife."

As the first ill-fated employee walked into my office that day, I made no small talk. "I've asked you into my office to tell you that I'm going to let you go." I paused, allowing the words to sink in. "I'm terribly sorry, but I have no choice."

My heart was pounding in my head. My throat was as dry as powder. I held my breath. Suddenly, without warning, the employee I was speaking to became a person. I had made no attempt at soft-selling the inevitable. I had spoken the truth in love. Somehow they seemed grateful.

Driving home that afternoon, completely exhausted, I breathed a prayer of gratitude for my family's help. I understand that sometimes diplomacy is unkind and manipulative. Best of all, I had learned something at home that became extremely valuable at work. Tender candor—not diplomacy—had won the day. My wife and kids were right.

Robert Wolgemuth has held executive positions in the publishing business, including the presidency of Thomas Nelson Communications and the chairmanship of a company he co-founded, Wolgemuth & Hyatt Publishers. He is the author of the best-selling books: She Calls Me Daddy; Pray with Me Daddy; The Devotional Bible for Dads; Daddy@Work. He and his wife, Bobbie, have two adult daughters, two sons-in-law, and two precious grandchildren. For more information on being a great dad, visit his website at www.HeyDad.com.

WHY THERE IS NO SUBSTITUTE FOR PARENTS

by Wade Horn, M.D.

Our culture has accepted the idea that fathers are superfluous—in other words, they are not necessary in the "modern" family.

In 1960, the total number of children living in fatherless families was fewer than eight million. Today, the total has risen to nearly twenty-four million. Nearly four out of ten children in America are being raised in homes without their fathers and soon it may be six out of ten. How did this happen? Why are so many of our nation's children growing up without a full-time father? It is because our culture has accepted the idea that fathers are superfluous—in other words, they are not necessary in the "modern" family. Supposedly, their contributions to the well-being of children can easily be performed by the state, which disburses welfare checks, subsidizes midnight basketball leagues, and establishes child-care facilities.

Ideas, of course, have consequences. And the consequences of this idea have been as profound as they have been disastrous. Almost 75 percent of American children living in fatherless households will experience poverty before the age of eleven, compared to only 20 percent of those raised by two parents. Children living in homes where fathers are absent are far more likely to be expelled from or drop out of school, develop emotional or behavioral problems, commit suicide, and fall victim to child abuse or neglect. The males are also far more likely to become violent criminals. As a matter of fact, men who grew up without dads currently represent 70 percent of the prison population serving long-term sentences.

Undeniably, fathers are important for the well-being of children. So, too, are traditional families. They ensure the continuity of civilization by propagating the species and socializing children. Everyone seems to understand the obvious benefits of propagation, but the important role that parents play in socializing children is widely misunderstood and undervalued.

The Process of Socialization

Socialization can be defined as the process whereby individuals acquire the behavior, attitudes, and values that are not only regarded as desirable and appropriate by society but that have also stood the test of time and proved to be the most humane. Proper socialization requires delaying or inhibiting "impulse gratification" in order to abide by the rule of law and the rule of custom. Well-socialized children have learned, for example, not to strike out at others to get what they want; poorly socialized children have not. Well-socialized children have learned to obey the directions of legitimate authority figures like parents and teachers; poorly socialized children have not. Well-socialized children have learned to cooperate and share with others; poorly socialized children have not.

Much of what is described as "good character" or "virtue" reflects the ability to delay or inhibit impulse gratification. When a child tells the truth, even though he knows that it will result in negative consequences, he is inhibiting the impulse to lie to avoid unpleasantness. When he shows charity to others, he is inhibiting the impulse to behave selfishly. A civil society is dependent upon virtuous citizens who have developed this capacity to delay or inhibit impulse gratification; that is, persons who can control their behavior voluntarily. Without a majority of such citizens, storekeepers would have to post armed guards in front of every display counter, women would live in constant fear of being raped by roaming bands of marauding men, and children would be left to the mercy of those who would exploit them. Fortunately, well-socialized children generally become well-socialized adults. Unfortunately, poorly socialized children generally do not. There are few statements one can make with complete certitude, but here is one: When families fail in their task to socialize children, a civil society is not possible. Herein lies the awesome responsibility of parenting.

Parents socialize children through two mechanisms. The first is teaching through direct instruction reinforced by a combination of rewards and punishments for acceptable and unacceptable behavior. The second is teaching by example. Of the two, the latter is the more important mechanism since most complex human behavior is acquired through observational learning. Children are much more likely to do as a parent does than as a parent says. This is why parents who lie and cheat tend to raise children who lie and cheat, despite any direct instruction to the contrary. As Benjamin Franklin once observed, the best sermon is indeed a good example.

Please note that I have not asserted that the state— or as it is euphemistically referred to these days, the "village"—is necessary for the proper socialization of children. Rather, it is parents who are necessary, and this means a mother and a father. There are, of course, thousands of single mothers who are doing a heroic job parenting and beating the odds. I do not mean to denigrate their efforts. Yet there is a great deal of hard evidence to suggest that when fathers are absent, boys tend to develop poor conduct. They "act out" their aggressive impulses, sometimes quite violently, toward others. Girls also tend to act out when fathers are absent, but in a different way; they become rebellious and promiscuous.

The Importance of Mothers and Fathers

No matter what the advocates of "gender-free parenting" say, mothers and fathers do parent differently. Mothers tend to be more verbal, whereas fathers are more physical. Mothers also tend to encourage personal safety and caution, whereas fathers are more challenging when it comes to achievement, independence and risk-taking. And mothers tend to be stronger comforting figures than fathers who are more intent upon establishing and enforcing rules governing the behavior of their children.

The fact that mothers and fathers parent differently is not to say that one group does it "right" or "better" than the other. What children need to develop good character is the combination of what mothers and fathers bring to the parenting equation. Take the fact that mothers tend to be nurturers and fathers tend to be disciplinarians. Parenting experts used to believe that families socialize children best when both parents adopt a nurturing but permissive role, demonstrating high levels of love and low levels of control Decades of research have shown, however, that when children are reared this way they act out through chronic bad behavior.

Permissiveness as a "parenting style" simply doesn't work. Boys and girls need a high level of nurturing balanced by a high level of control. Those who are reared in families that exhibit this combination are friendlier, more energetic, and better behaved. Those who are reared by single mothers, therefore, are warm and affectionate but have difficulty learning self-discipline. Conversely, those who are reared by single fathers are obedient but often are often plagued by anxiety and insecurity.

It has also been fashionable for those pushing for gender-free parenting to assert that the physical play of fathers has no beneficial impact on child rearing. Many self-proclaimed child experts exhort fathers to stop playing with the kids and do more housework. Some even claim that the rough-and-tumble play of fathers teaches aggression and should be avoided. But new clinical studies reveal that the physical play of fathers actually gives children much-needed practice in regulating their emotions and behavior and helps them develop the capacity to recognize the emotional cues of others.

The point is not to force a choice between the parenting role of mothers or fathers but to suggest that they work best when they work together. This view contrasts sharply with the "two pair of hands" argument, which holds that when it comes to parenting, two people are better than one and it makes no difference whether they are mothers or fathers. In reality it matters greatly to whom the "two pairs of hands" are attached. Kids don't need impersonal "caregivers;" they need loving moms and dads.

Fathers are also critical to the proper socialization of children because they teach by example how to keep negative impulses in check. It is through boys' observation of the way their fathers deal with frustrations, anger, and sadness that they learn how men should cope with such emotions. It is also through the observation of how fathers treat mothers that boys learn how men should treat women. if fathers treat mothers with dignity and respect, then it is likely that their sons will grow up to treat women with dignity and respect. If fathers treat mothers with contempt and cruelty, then it is likely that their sons will, too. Fathers are also critical for the healthy emotional development of girls. If girls experience the love, attention, and protection of fathers, then they are likely to resist the temptations of seeking such things elsewhere—often through casual sexual relations at a very young age. Finally, fathers are important in helping children make the difficult transition to the adult world. Boys require an affirmation that they are "man enough." Girls require an affirmation that they are "worthy enough."

Given this understanding, what should we expect when fatherlessness becomes the norm? We don't need a crystal ball to find the answer. As I indicated earlier, nearly four out of every ten children are being raised absent their fathers right now. The result is that juveniles are the fastest growing segment of the criminal population in the United States. Between 1982 and 1991, the rate at which children were arrested for murder increased 93 percent; for aggravated assault, 72 percent; for rape, 24 percent; and for automobile theft, 97 percent. Although homicide rates have increased for all ages, those for teenagers have increased more rapidly than for adults.

The teen population is expected to grow by 20 percent over the next decade, and this is precisely the generation most likely to be reared without fathers. The prospect has led many sociologists, criminologists, and law enforcement agencies to conclude that shortly after the turn of the century we will see an adolescent crime wave the likes of which has never been seen before in this country. If that were not enough, we know that each and every day:

> 7,700 children become sexually active;
> 1,100 children have abortions;
> 2,500 children are born out of wedlock;
> 600 children contract syphilis or gonorrhea;
> and six children commit suicide.

Fatherlessness is not solely responsible for these tragedies, but it certainly is a major cause. Indeed, all the available evidence suggests that improving the well-being of our children—and ultimately our nation—depends upon finding ways to bring fathers back into the home. The question is: How?

The Fatherhood Solution

First, our culture needs to replace the idea of the superfluous father with a more compelling understanding of the critical role fathers play in the lives of their children, not just as "paychecks," but as disciplinarians, teachers, and moral guides. And fathers must be physically present in the home. They can't simply show up on the weekends or for pre-arranged "quality time." Children need to know that their fathers are literally there for them.

Second, we need to convey the importance and sanctity of marriage. While most boys and girls expect that they will eventually get married and have children, they no longer believe that there needs to be a chronology to these two events. They should be taught that marriage comes first and that it is not a trial arrangement that can be abandoned whenever conflicts arise. Here's where religious and moral instruction can make a huge difference, because children need to know that marriage is far more than a state-approved contract between two parties or a box to check on an income tax return.

Third, we must make restoring the rights and responsibilities of parents a national priority. Over the past century, child rearing has increasingly come to be viewed as a public rather than a private matter. As early as 1901, the Supreme Court of Indiana upheld a compulsory education law by arrogantly declaring, "the natural rights of a parent to the custody and control of his children are subordinate to the power of the state." The assault on parental authority gradually extended to all other areas of life. By 1960, one social worker writing in the prestigious professional journal, Child Welfare, felt free to note that "day care can offer something valuable to children because they are separated from their parents." [Emphasis added.] School-based condom distribution, "witch hunts" against parents suspected of abuse without sufficient cause, abortion on demand without parental consent—these are all contemporary examples of how the state has chosen to wage war against parents and convince children that the very people they count on most in this world are out to hurt them. In essence, the state is saying to today's children, "Do not trust your parents—we don't."

The tide is turning, however. Even many die-hard critics of the traditional family have finally been forced to admit that their ivory tower theories are wrong; in the real world, children need to be raised by two parents. And parents need the freedom to decide what is in the best interest of their own children. Another positive development is the "pro-family movement" that has grown tremendously in the last few years. There are now dozens of national and regional organizations dedicated to championing parental initiatives. And pro-family rallies have attracted stadium-size crowds around the country.

What can you do right now in your own home and your own community? You can start by pledging, "I will be a good wife and mother," or, "I will be a good husband and father." It is a simple promise, to be sure. But it is a promise upon which a good, just, and civil society depends.

Reprinted by permission from IMPRIMIS, the monthly journal of Hillsdale College.

Wade F. Horn, PhD, is president of National Fatherhood Initiative, an organization whose mission is to reinstate fatherhood as a national priority. The National Fatherhood Initiative is working to deploy a national work force for the purpose of restoring the meaning of, and personal commitment to, fatherhood.

Motivating Change

Success is more than a name, it's everything!

Zig Ziglar

Success Is More Than A Name, It's Everything!

Zig Ziglar has one of the most recognized names in America, but he has come to know success as more than a name.

by Brian Mast

Many years ago, while attending a family reunion in his hometown of Yazoo City, Mississippi, Zig Ziglar bought several items at a local store. After his wife wrote the check, she pulled out her driver's license for identification, but the cashier stopped her, saying, "No need for that. Around here the name 'Ziglar' is all the identification we need."

That respect was based on the reputation built by his mother and his older brothers and sisters still living in the area. At that point, Ziglar promised himself again that if he never left his children a dime he would leave them a name that would be "all the identification they would need." Today he is grateful he has both to pass on to his children.

Growing Up at the End of the Line

Growing up in the heart of the Great Depression helped to shape Ziglar's life. The 10th of 12 children, his father died when Zig was five, leaving his mother with six children too small to be gainfully employed. The family survived because they had five cows, a large garden, and two older brothers who were periodically able to get part-time day jobs to buy staples from the grocery store.

Young Ziglar was helping around the home by age four, and milking cows before he was eight. All the siblings worked hard, but nothing compared to his mother. "She'd get up early, cook breakfast on a wood stove, and then get us ready for the day. Many times I'd get up in the night and she'd be quilting in the hallway (that's where there was light) or altering and patching our clothes."

His mother worked hard to keep the family going, and Ziglar adds, "She was not only the hardest-working person I've ever known, but she was probably the wisest person I've ever known." Though she had only a fifth grade education, her insight helped shape Ziglar's thinking. Even at a young age he remembers noticing that some children had things he didn't have, but he was grateful for a loving mother who had great faith and raised her children on hard work and character.

While in school, Ziglar was not a model student. "I'm a good student now," he says, in reference to the fact that he has been reading an average of three hours each day for the past 26 years. Between the 11th and 12th grades he attended Hinds Junior College in Raymond, Mississippi, to take advanced algebra and a class in American history. The history class, it turned out, was to be a turning point in his life.

The teacher, Coach Joby Harris, taught with such enthusiasm that Ziglar decided to major in history when he went to college. Coach Harris did more than teach history; he showed Ziglar that he had a destiny and an obligation to fulfill it. Harris said, "If you have an ability that goes beyond providing for your own needs, you have an obligation to reach down and lift up those who can't meet their own needs. If you don't," Coach warned in the summer of 1943, "they, by the sheer weight of their numbers, will reach up and pull you down." These words deeply impacted Ziglar who now says, "We are seeing his prophecy fulfilled."

But there was more than a summer of history in store for Ziglar. When Coach Harris was a boy, his Boy Scout Master was Thomas B. Abernathy, the first Scout official in Mississippi. Mr. Abernathy taught Joby Harris scouting and even more as a mentor. Mr. Abernathy had three daughters and a son. His youngest daughter, Jean, in November of 1999, will have been Mrs. Zig Ziglar for 52 years.

Becoming a Top Performer

The road to success was long and often bumpy for Ziglar, but he was persistent. He and Jean married in 1946 and a year later he started selling Wearever Aluminum Cookware. After two and a half years of struggling, he attended a training session conducted by visiting Tennessee supervisor P. C. Merrell. "You have the ability to become the national champion and later an executive in the company if you will only recognize your ability and go to work on an organized schedule." Because of Mr. Merrell's integrity and the fact that he had written the sales training program, Ziglar believed what he said and within a year he was the no two salesman out of 7,000 sales people in the company. Then, in 1952 his dream to become a speaker was born when he heard Bob Bale, a motivational speaker from Phoenix, Arizona, speak at a seminar in Florence, South Carolina.

Success as a motivational speaker did not come quickly or easily to Ziglar, who admits, "For 16 years I struggled desperately to get speaking engagements, and supported my family by continuing my sales career." He credits his wife, whom he lovingly refers to as "The

Redhead," with encouraging him to continue. Today he says that having a cheerleader cheering him on every day and praying for him every night is what made the difference in those early, struggling years. Her love and encouragement keep him fired up today.

In 1972, Ziglar found what he had been missing all along. It was July 4th when an elderly African American woman spent the weekend at the Ziglar home. She walked in talking about Jesus Christ and she talked about Jesus all the time she was there. As a result, Ziglar committed his life to Christ. Although Zigler was raised in a Christian home and attended church most of his life, he had never had a personal relationship with Jesus Christ. That weekend he surrendered his life to Jesus and His purposes for his life.

At age 45, Ziglar had a new beginning and the ultimate love and power source. He had tried for 45 years to make it happen his way, but he was broken and in debt. "I had exhausted my own ego, I knew I didn't have the answers, and I needed help," he candidly says. "I think God let me struggle for years so that when things did happen, there would be no question as to who made it happen." Shortly after his conversion and commitment, including tithing, Ziglar was suddenly hit with a $600 per week engagement. "Soon after, General Mills called with a request that I do a series of seminars and they wanted to pay me in advance to get it in that year's budget." This had never happened before, so Ziglar knew he was experiencing the "unexplainable" provision of God.

Since 1972, Ziglar has not had to solicit a single speaking engagement. For 26 straight years he has had to turn down engagements because his calendar has been full. Ziglar clearly understands Who is in charge and is glad it's not him!

Ziglar's business continues to grow. Today, he is Chairman of Ziglar Training Systems, based in Carrollton, Texas, which employs 37+ trained individuals and offers sales, motivation and customer service training programs to multiple companies and agencies. In 1998, Ziglar had "only" 50 public engagements, which allows him more time to write. He has written 14 books, nine of which have become best sellers.

Mixing Faith in the Workplace

"Americans are religious by nature," Ziglar says. He points out that on any Sunday there are more people in church than at every NBA, NFL and Major League Baseball game for the entire year combined.

Ziglar explains, "I bring my faith into my presentations by explaining that I validate things psychologically, theologically and physiologically before I write, record or verbalize them. People say you shouldn't talk about the spiritual, but I say, 'I'm gonna talk about it because you are going to be dead a whole lot longer than you'll be alive, so it is important to make some long-range goals.'"

He makes friends with his audiences, which is very important, he explains, "because you seldom get upset with someone who has had you laughing." As he continues to speak, he explains to the audience that everything they think or believe needs to be validated— he brings up quantifiable statistics from studies that show, for example, that families who regularly go to a place of worship have fewer divorces, nervous breakdowns, alcoholism, etc., and even make more money than those who don't attend worship services.

Although a lot of what he says is food for thought—at least he gets them thinking. He notes that his tape series, "Christian Motivation for Daily Living," is the biggest selling single set of tapes they offer at public seminars. "People are genuinely interested in the spiritual aspects of life," he explains.

Sometimes it is the little things that make the big impact. Whenever he autographs books, he always signs his name and writes a Bible verse beside it. People come to him later and say, "When you signed my book, I went home and read the Scripture you wrote. I got into my Bible and now I'm a Christian," or "I got back into church." Ziglar points out, "This has happened hundreds of times."

When it comes right down to it, he knows what he is saying is practical, true and helpful. He explains, "I thought I loved my wife before I got married, but I discovered I didn't have a clue of what it meant to love someone until I learned to love through Christ." He talks with his audiences about the personal, family, and business challenges that are common to every individual, and how to handle those challenges. The audiences love it and come back for more.

On the personal side, he has had to walk out his faith in his home as well. His firstborn was an "intellectual type," says Ziglar, and she didn't want anything to do with his newfound faith. He wrote *Confessions of a Happy Christian* with the intent to win her to Christ, but initially she didn't read it. However, after a business friend witnessed to her and her husband, she started to read it and told him she "had never seen so much joy jump off the pages of a book." A few days later, during a Sunday afternoon visit, she still told her father, "Daddy, I'm just not ready."

Ziglar says that it broke his heart, but he knew he shouldn't pursue it further at that moment. Then, eight days later, Ziglar was speaking at an event and afterwards she came up to him and said, "Daddy, I'm glad you met Jesus when you did, because if you hadn't met Him then, I wouldn't know Him now."

Ziglar still tears up when he relates the story, but he is overjoyed to know that all four of his children came to know Christ as their Lord and Savior and are truly successful in every sense of the word.

A balanced success is within reach of virtually everyone, Ziglar believes, yet most people develop only a fraction of their potential. The potential factor is what gets him so excited, as he is quick to note, "If man can take moldy bread and make penicillin out of it, then just think what an awesome God can make out of a man or woman He created in His own image!"

Zig Ziglar is himself a walking testimony of what he believes. That is why he continues to say, "There is no question in my mind as to why I am where I am today."

Race Driver Goes Clean

by Bob Harrison

Stock car driver Darrell Waltrip announced the changing of his race car team sponsorship. He dropped a beer company and signed up with a laundry detergent company as a new sponsor.

People live their lives according to their own self-image and the image others hold of them. One man who knows about image is stock car driver...

Darrell Waltrip

I came across a short story about Waltrip changing sponsorship, and more importantly, why he decided to do so.

Shortly after he miraculously survived a Daytona 500 crash, he began attending church with his wife. A new joy and purpose entered his life.

One day as he and his wife were visiting with their pastor, the minister asked, "I notice that your car is sponsored by a beer company. Is that the image you want to portray for yourself?"

The issue was not beer drinking, it was the kind of image that this type of sponsorship would create for him.

Darrell thought about it. He did care about his image. He thought, "If our prayers for a child are answered, what kind of dad do I want to be? What kind of image do I want my son or daughter to have of me?"

An opportunity opened for him to sign with a new racing team sponsored by a laundry detergent company! Remembering his pastor's admonition to walk the walk, not just talk the talk, he decided to switch teams.

Two years later, daughter Jessica was born, and a few years later, daughter Sarah. In 1989, Darrell won the premier race of the stock car circuit—the Daytona 500.

Waltrip changed sponsors when he got hold of the principle that our lives and our image replicate themselves in the lives of others. We must remember: we are an example to others, especially our own children.

Little Children Follow Me
A careful man I must be,
Little children follow me.
I do not dare go astray,
For they will go the self-same way.

I cannot escape their watchful eye,
Whatever they see me do, they'll try.
Like me they say they're going to be,
Little children who follow me.

I must remember as I go,
Through summer suns and winter snows,
As I am building, for the years to be,
That little children follow me.

Unknown

Would you be willing for someone to videotape your personal life and then use that tape as a training device for others?

"It were better for him that a millstone were hanged about his neck, and he cast into the sea, than that he should offend one of these little ones." Luke 17:2

Bob Harrison is a successful author, business owner and dynamic speaker. Used with permission from Power Points for Success by Bob Harrison. Copyright ©1997 Honor Books Publishers.

Unconventional
Leadership

Michael Landes

Unconventional Leadership

For Michael Landes, businessman and mayor, doing nothing is more difficult than sacrificing to help others.

by Eileen O'Gorman

In the ears of today's business world, Michael Landes' ideas sound radical. His actions shake the world's business norms at their very foundation and cause ripple effects that are reformational. And we should expect nothing less, for the message that Michael Landes communicates is inspired by the One who challenges the misconceptions of any age and offers truth that transforms public and private life, business and politics. Landes, in short, is a man with an entrepreneurial spirit, seeing opportunities to use his talents for God's glory.

As a young business innovator, Landes has dealt with success from the beginning. He helped create Tennis Agents International, an organization that set up tennis schools in Europe, and eventually landed in the resort community of Indian Wells. While considering whether or not to pursue a degree in business from one of the nation's top business schools, Landes and his wife faced what they would later see as the first of many challenges to operate according to biblical priorities and trust the Lord for the results. Because they believed a life on the business fast-track would involve too great a sacrifice for the family they envisioned having, they took an alternate route, not knowing what lay ahead.

Michael and his wife Stephanie founded Convention Cassettes Unlimited (CCU) in 1987. CCU has become one of the largest on-site recording companies in the nation. Although Michael now serves as chairman of this convention recording company, his leadership is anything but conventional.

Serving Christ in Business

Looking back, Landes can see that the Lord gave him a desire to work as an entrepreneur. "When I first got into business, I didn't understand what the term 'call' meant," says Landes. "I'm not even sure I ever felt that I was a businessman. But God gave me an entrepreneurial spirit and a business that was entrepreneurial in nature.

"I believe the Lord gave me this opportunity and the calling to 'run with it,' but not in order to create a context in which we made a lot of money and gratified all of our employee needs as well as our own family needs. That's not what this is about. It's about a call to be a servant and to bring God's principles into the marketplace."

Landes warns against a money-driven mentality in the business arena. "Business people need to be open to asking themselves on Monday morning, 'What am I doing to change my community and help it become more closely linked to God's cause and not the world's causes?' This question must replace the standard, 'What can I do to make more money?' If Christians accept the challenge of this question we can make an impact on our country."

Landes takes these challenges seriously for himself and for his company. The result is a business philosophy that stands in stark contrast to commonly accepted practices. "We need to be willing to sacrifice profit, overhead, and personnel in order to give of ourselves and our money to Christian and even non-Christian programs that benefit our culture and community in accord with biblical priorities," says Landes. "We can't expect to change people or programs unless we are willing to sacrifice ourselves."

Landes' corporation practically flushes out these ideas through service and financial support given to local organizations that help people in a variety of situations. For example, the entire customer service department—personnel and phones—is donated annually to help a local organization provide Thanksgiving Day meals for the needy.

Against the Current

Landes and his attitudes may seem a little out of place coming from a resident of one of the richest communities in the United States. He may sound even more out of place considering that in recent years, as the city of Indian Wells has grown richer, little has been done to help surrounding communities in the Coachella Valley.

"We were the wealthiest city in the Valley, but at the same time we were giving nothing back to the community in terms of money, time, effort and sacrifice," Landes says. "People made decisions based on how they benefited the three thousand people of Indian Wells rather than how they benefited the 250,000 people of the Valley. We had reserves in the millions, and Indian Wells was only giving to about six of the one-hundred plus charities in the Valley."

It is because of Landes' belief that Christians can impact their culture that he took a personal stand and became involved in a mission to help needy people in the Coachella Valley and eventually pursued service in local politics.

A "Social Entrepreneur"

Landes naturally applies his entrepreneurial skills to community renewal and reform. He calls it being a "social entrepreneur." "All ideas are grassroots ideas," he says. "Whether it be opposing abortion or working to bring biblically-based values to your community, you begin on the small level, start small. Then you start working up and it grows. That's what an entrepreneur does."

Landes started small by joining the Coachella Valley Rescue Mission Board. He describes this mission as "the only group in our area that was sharing with the homeless, not only helping sustain them, but requiring them to be sustained by the Spirit of God." Landes applied the experience he had as a business entrepreneur to the work of the rescue mission, helping it become a solid and growing program that proclaims the message of the gospel.

Standing for Christ in Politics

As Landes' involvement in the mission grew, his awareness of what Indian Wells could do to serve the entire Coachella Valley grew as well. In hopes of changing the direction of Indian Wells, Landes entered local politics in 1996. In 1997, he was elected mayor.

How did Landes and his biblical stands make their way into the highest elected office in the city? Did he have to compromise his views in order to gain acceptance? Landes opted for another way, and his advice is this: "If you are convinced that the most critical thing in your life is your relationship with Jesus Christ, then don't dilute that—from the very beginning," says Landes. "We must be wise as serpents and gentle as doves. And whatever comes your way—the questions, the issues and controversies—resolve the conflicts based on your own prayers and supplications. Then let the chips fall. If people elect you, then I think you need to feel compelled that you were supposed to be there."

Leading by Following

Landes readily admits that success in any area brings the temptation to believe that intimacy with Christ is not necessary. "For instance, if you are elected mayor, people will come up to you and say 'Mr. Mayor' and jokingly bow down to you. But you begin to think in your mind, 'Gee, I'm pretty neat stuff aren't I?' You cannot let ego and pride get in there because it is a lie and it will break you."

"If you are a Christian in a leadership position, join with your peers and have a Bible study. Talk about your challenges and weaknesses. This is a crucial part of being a leader. You are in a challenging position because you are naturally a leader. But we must constantly understand what Christ meant about being a servant."

The imagery of the vine and the branches helps Landes remember the reality of the opportunities he has been given to serve. The great leader, he says, is the one who is a follower. "As a Christian business leader what can you do to impact your culture?" Landes asks. "Become a follower. Ask yourself, 'Where does God want me? What does He want me to do?'"

The first place to ask these questions, Landes says, is at home. "I have to ask if I am doing the right thing at home for Christ before I ask if I am doing the right thing in business. Trusting Christ's leadership will often show you areas where you're not living as you should be, and that's when you have to remind yourself that you are not the one in control."

Trusting the Lord

Raising a family, being a husband, and balancing work and mayoral responsibilities make Landes a busy man. He's found that the only way to achieve balance is to take his life before the Lord each day. "It's part of our culture to be sort of spinning out of control," Landes says.

"At the end of the day I have to go before God and ask Him to give me balance. I have to trust Him with decisions and then I have to give up control of the outcomes."

"A verse that encourages me and that I think any person in business can hang on to is I Peter 1:13: 'Therefore, prepare your minds for action; be self-controlled; set your hope fully on the grace to be given you when Jesus Christ is revealed.' That verse reminds me that God knows me and that He has plans for me. How much better this is than simply grabbing the latest book promising *The Ten Best Ways to Step Out in the Community and Get Ahead.*"

Reprinted from Leader to Leader by permission of Covenant Theological Seminary and Eileen O'Gorman, St. Louis, Missouri.

Exercise Your Rights Control Your Time

By John Mason

Don't ask time where it's gone; tell it where to go

All great achievers, all successful people, are those who have been able to gain control over their time. It has been said that all human beings have been created equal in one respect: each person has been given 24 hours each day.

We need to choose to give our best time to our most challenging situation. It's not how much we do that matters; it's how much we get done. We should choose to watch our time, not our watch.

Don't spend a dollar's worth of time for ten cent's worth of results.

Make sure to take care of the vulnerable times in your days. These vulnerable times are the first thing in the morning and the last thing at night. I have heard a minister say that what a person is like at midnight when he is all alone reveals that person's true self.

Never allow yourself to say, "I could be doing big things if I weren't so busy doing small things!" or "I'd give anything to be able to..." Take control of your time. The greater control you exercise over your time, the greater freedom you will experience in your life.

The psalmist prayed, "So teach us to number our days, that we may apply our hearts unto wisdom" (Ps. 90:12). The Bible teaches us that the devil comes to steal, and to kill, and to destroy (John 10:10), and this verse applies to time as well as to people. The enemy desires to provide God's children with ideas of how to kill, steal, and destroy valuable time. One of the best time savers is the ability to say no. Learn to say "No"— not saying no when you should is one of the biggest wastes of time you will ever experience.

There is a basic leadership principle that says, "6 x 1 = 6." If you want to write a book, learn to play a musical instrument, become a better tennis player, or do anything else important, you should devote one hour a day, six days a week, to the project. Sooner than you think, what you desire will become a reality. A person can accomplish many things in 312 hours a year! A commitment of one hour a day, six days a week, is all it takes.

The differences between people are determined by what they do with the amount of time at their disposal. Don't be like the airline pilot flying over the Pacific Ocean who reported to his passengers, "We're lost, but we're making great time!" Remember that the future arrives an hour at a time. Gain control of your time, and you will gain control of your life!

Did you know you have exactly the same number of hours per day that were given to Leonardo da Vinci,

Michangelo, Thomas Jefferson, Louis Pasteur, Helen Keller, Albert Einstein and Mother Theresa?

Exercise Your Rights—Control Your Time!

The Dreamer
Behind the
Dreams

Dexter Yager

The Dreamer behind the Dreams

by Brian Mast

When Dexter Yager was first introduced to Amway in 1964, he was making $95 a week and his wife was expecting their fifth child. Their Amway business grew quickly but soon leveled off. "My dream was too small," he recalls. So Dexter enlarged his vision and moved his family from their tiny home on the alley in Rome, New York to Charlotte, North Carolina. From that point onwards, there has been no looking back.

Today, Dexter runs a multimillion dollar business and is a much sought after motivational speaker. At first glance it would appear that he has "arrived," but he would never agree. One part of success, he says, "is continually moving forwards toward the next dream." He has, however, arrived at a level where most people, critics and admirers alike, must sit up and take notice.

Dexter speaks out: About Himself

Regardless of what he says, Dexter is not an average guy. Consider his schedule. He wakes up late in the afternoon and typically spends several hours meeting with other businessmen or counseling top distributors in his massive organization. He often counsels and responds to voice mail from his distributors until 3 or 4 a.m. before going to bed. Why such an extreme schedule? His pace demands it. Every weekend he flies to a convention where he speaks for several hours on Friday, Saturday, and sometimes on Sunday. His wife Birdie also speaks, mostly during the Sunday morning church services, a mainstay at all the Yager functions.

At most speaking engagements Dexter is the grand finale, regularly speaking from 11 p.m. until 2 or 3 in the morning to tens of thousands of people. Though few would believe it, he used to be quiet and shy, often stuttering through his presentations. In fact, when he was in school he used to skip class to avoid giving oral book reports. Now, he says with a smile, "I don't leave time for silence. I apologize, but I don't change."

Personal Battle

His schedule is physically demanding and Dexter does his best to take care of himself. With his wife's encouragement, he has lost 65 pounds over the last three years, going from a 43 inch to a 34 inch waist. "I used to eat more than my fare share of ice cream," he admits, "and it almost cost me my life."

Almost 13 years ago he suffered a major stroke. His entire right side was paralyzed and eight neurologists told him he would be confined to a wheelchair and never walk again. He refused to accept the doctors' diagnosis, however, and after years of hard work retraining his body, he now exercises daily and walks without a limp. "My whole right side was shot," he recalls, "and I was forced to become left-handed after 48 years." When people ask him about his stroke, he replies, "I ignored my health. I did it to myself. I thank God that He let me live through my stupidity." He works hard to keep his body conditioned, practicing what he preaches, "You will eventually win if you keep trying."

Speaking before as many as 75,000 people at once, Dexter simply does what comes naturally for him. "I'm not a professional speaker," he says. "When I get up there, I don't know what I'm going to say half the time, but I try to encourage them in their life,"

Dexter has several honorary degrees hanging on the wall at his home in North Carolina, but his favorite is his "MBA" degree. His good friend, Dave Thomas (founder of Wendy's restaurants), awarded him the degree several years ago. "MBA" stands for "Mop Bucket Award," an award given to men who are willing to clean the floors, thus classifying them as management material. Though he never went to college, his background of serving others, working hard, and managing people has made Dexter one of the most prominent leaders in Amway.

Turning Point

His relationship with God has always been an important part of Dexter's life. In fact, at one time he felt he was called to start his own church, despite his rapidly growing Amway business. He prayed about the decision until one night an evangelist told him that he would one day "have one of the largest ministries in the business world." Three different confirmations from different people, all saying he was in the right place doing the right thing, helped convince him that he was to pursue his original vision to be the most successful businessman he could be with all his energy. He didn't believe it would just happen, however. He knew he had to put the dream of having a large business out in front of him and get to work.

Today, Dexter's business employs over 400 people in Charlotte, North Carolina, whose sole purpose is to supply support to his downline. They recently merged two of their largest Amway related businesses under one roof, a massive 377,000 sq. foot building. Intercontinental Communication Corporation of America (ICCA) and International Network Services (InterNET) are housed in the new facility. ICCA produces millions audio cassettes each year as well as hundreds of thousands of video tapes and music tracks. InterNET operates as a service to the hundreds of thousands of Amway distributors in Dexter's downline, supplying them with the "tools" they need to be successful. Capable individuals and family members, principally his children, are responsible for the daily management of his ever-expanding business.

About Family

"You can spoil your mate, but not your kids," explains Dexter. He has done his best to prepare his seven children for the future. Preparation, he admits, requires a lot of work and he has given his life for his family. Dexter included his children in his business whenever he could with the intent of someday passing to them the responsibility of taking his business into the next generation. His philosophy is to "load them with responsibility," thus equipping them with a strong work ethic and an understanding of personal commitment. "The second generation," he explains, "has to prove it another way."

His training has paid off, sometimes to his surprise. Dexter once hired a former bank president to secure loans for future construction work. But after six months, not a single loan had been arranged. One of his sons approached Dexter and said, "If I can get you the loans, can we eliminate his position?" Dexter had the loans by noon the next day, and his son, then age 18, had another responsibility.

Three of his sons are responsible for InterNET and are expanding the business beyond what he had ever imagined. They are also involved in several other businesses and are, at Dexter's last count, the presidents of over 30 corporations. Dexter's brother, Butch, runs Yager Construction, a multimillion dollar business based in Charlotte that builds for Yager Enterprises as well as other outside projects. Amway has provided the means for Dexter to "dabble" in real estate, apartment complexes, strip malls, office buildings, and numerous other ventures. To "dabble" is Dexter's way of saying, "I have more successful businesses than I want to mention."

His seven children have a strong relationship between themselves. Each month they get together, without Dexter or Birdie, to spend a day together. They understand, like their father, the importance of family. Dexter says he can't accept credit for the business success of his children, but he does accept credit for raising them.

About Work and Business

Having a successful business is no small accomplishment, but Dexter points out that, "keeping it is the real challenge." Dexter reached the level of Crown Ambassador, the highest level within Amway, in 1985. His business has grown in such large proportions that he says, "if we spent our time tracking it, we would not have time for anything else." He candidly adds that he doesn't know his net worth or how many high-selling distributors he has in his downline, but he doesn't want to know. His rule of thumb is, "I don't need to know. If I know how much I have, then I don't have enough."

Big Vision

His vision is to keep getting bigger and bigger. "Like a pastor," he explains, "if he doesn't have a building program, then he better have just completed one, otherwise it's the end." His joy in business comes from building, growing, and increasing, and he says, "That's where the fun is."

Owning his own business was always his goal and it has given him the freedom to be his own boss, but he quickly adds, "You have to enjoy working 80 to 100 hours for yourself." Liking his work has never been a problem for Dexter, especially since his family and many of his close friends are directly involved in his business.

Plain & Simple

Dexter says his home and guesthouse situated on a lake in North Carolina are simply "where we sleep." Although the entire estate took eight years to build at a cost of well over $6 million, the Yager's have a much lower percentage of their net worth tied up in housing than the average homeowner.

Dexter and Birdie, after being married for almost 42 years, love each other more than ever. Dexter seems to have life and all its frills in the proper perspective. The bottom line, he explains, is this: "When I die, I ain't gonna take none of it with me."

Some complain that Amway ralliesare all about money, which prompts Dexter to ask the question, "How many people get a new job and don't ask about their pay? You don't work for free, do you?" Money is the fruit of an individual's labor and is not a bad thing to talk about, regardless of what people say or think.

Dexter and Birdie support several charitable organizations including one of their favorites, an orphanage in Africa. Although people are always interested in how much money wealthy people give, Dexter isn't about to say. Once, a pastor asked him to tell the congregation how much he was giving to the church's building fund, he flatly declined. "I want my blessing to come from God, not from man."

About being a Christian in Business

Dexter believes "Christians ought to reflect success wherever they are, especially in business." Though he has received some criticism for his outspoken beliefs, he feels it is a price he has to pay and that God will bless him for it. In addition, he says Christians should be giving people and not make up the "majority in the welfare community." "Those who give are like sponges," he explains. "Others who hold what they have will rot, like a wet sponge in the sun, but those who give out will be able to absorb more and give more the next time."

Prayer is also an important ingredient for the Christian in business. Dexter started his business in prayer and today doesn't go out on stage without praying and asking God what to say. He says when he feels he does a "lousy" job, he gets the best comments back, but when he feels he does a great job, he says, "nobody tells me." He says that if it was good, it was God, but if it was bad, then it was all him.

Leading by Example

When it comes to being a true example in the work place, Dexter doesn't mince his words. "We (Christians) are to be the strength that everybody sees and our peacefulness and lifestyle should be attractive. Then others will be willing to listen to what we have to say about Jesus. Not only are Christians to be the example, they are supposed to be successful." This misunderstanding is an issue that Dexter feels very strongly about. After all, he points out, "We are supposed to be the salt of the earth."

Being a Christian in business does not guarantee success. Many mistakenly believe that if God wants them to succeed, the money will come in on its own. The truth of the matter is that the struggles and challenges in business are intended to make the individual grow. Dexter says, "If we don't struggle we can't learn and if we can't learn then we can't teach and if we can't teach and help everybody else, then we will never amount to anything."

Part of being successful is pursuing your dreams. Dexter candidly states, "If you don't have a dream, you're dead." Everyone needs a reason to get out of bed in the morning. Growing up in the 50's and 60's he would walk by a customized '47 Mercury convertible with a beautiful paint job, custom tail lights, and plush interior and say, "Someday." It was a dream, he points out, "but without a dream or vision, the Bible says that a man will perish."

Dexter's dream when he first started in Amway was to quit his job and have his own business. When he had accomplished that, in his mind he had arrived. "Arriving," he discovered, was his biggest possible downfall. He realized his dreams were too small, much like the small-town mentality he had growing up. When he learned to expand his dreams, life and business took on a new meaning for Dexter. Now he says, "I know I have to be a dreamer and teach other people how to dream."

Little dreams grow into larger dreams, but as Dexter explains, "You have to start someplace." Some people find it hard to believe that such a successful man came from such humble beginnings. "We started so many times and in so many places to get to this point," Dexter points out, "and where we are now is only the starting point to get to the next point."

The Truth of the Matter

Many people have approached Dexter and said that they would get in the Amway business if they could start where he is. To which he replies, "I didn't start here! If I don't build a house with my own hands, I certainly wouldn't be able to repair it myself. I have to know how to build it. The same applies in business."

Dexter is well aware that there is a price to pay for building dreams and accomplishing goals. He has overcome his share of fears and discouragement in every area of his life to achieve the success he has today. He has learned over the years not to let the small things get in his way. In his relentless quest to help others achieve their dreams, his biggest challenge has been to convince people that they are worthy to receive all God has for them. But they must dream big. "Remember," says Dexter, "without a dream a man will perish."

THE TRUE CHRISTIAN ENTREPRENEUR
By A.L. Andrews

The Calling of the Christian
Entrepreneur

What is an entrepreneur? According to *Webster's New World Dictionary*, it is "a person who organizes and manages a business undertaking, assuming the risk for the sake of profit." The current popular view often provides a little more color to this description. Some include adjectives like: independent, self confident (even arrogant), loner, innovative, motivated, self-starter, profit-oriented, cunning, shrewd, and others.

How does this compare with the Christian entrepreneur? Let's take a look at Webster's definition in a biblical light.

A Business Undertaking:

The first and foremost issue, for the Christian entrepreneur, must be that God is the force behind the dream, drive and diligence for whatever business undertaking he may pursue. The true Christian entrepreneur has a calling to the business arena. The desire for organizing and managing a business comes from God and is not generated simply by need, present opportunity, or individual aspiration.

"Unless the Lord builds the house, its builders labor in vain" (Psalm 127:1).

Anyone can start and operate a business and even have a measure of success. Not everyone, however, is called by God and directed by the Holy Spirit to be an entrepreneur. Scripture makes it vitally clear that not everyone has the same abilities and call. It is important to understand this before striking out on that great business undertaking.

"...Do not think of yourself more highly than you ought, but rather think of yourself with sober judgment, in accordance with the measure of faith God has given you...We have different gifts, according to the grace given us" (Romans 12: 3, 6).

You have been given a measure of faith to work with the gifts (abilities) given to you. If the business arena isn't where you are gifted and called, you must think "with sober judgment" about whether that is where you really want to be. Is it where you will be the most effective and fulfilled?

The world (Christians included, unfortunately) is filled with individuals who are miserable, trying desperately to do something they were neither called nor equipped to do. They labor at what was expected of them or what they thought would bring prosperity and fulfillment. In the process, they have held back from pursuing what may have really been on their heart to do—their God given dream.

"Again, it will be like a man going on a journey, who called his servants and entrusted his property to them. To one he gave five talents of money, to another two talents, and to

274

another one talent, each according to his ability" (Matthew 25:14-15).

God entrusts you with opportunities fitting with and according to your abilities. You will never truly flourish if you attempt something other than what God has called you to do. He knows your abilities and directs your steps accordingly. You must pursue the opportunity He has given you in order to hear those words we all desire to hear, "Well done good and faithful servant!"

"Do you see a man skilled in his work? He will serve before kings; he will not serve before obscure men" (Proverbs 22:29).

It is very apparent when you see skilled and trained people doing their job. They make it look easy and get superior results. God wants to show you off as you do what He has called you to do. When you apply your God given talents and abilities, you will stand out and be in demand.

Assuming the risk:

The entrepreneur, especially the Christian entrepreneur, sees opportunity where everyone else tends to see risk. The beauty of the life of the Christian entrepreneur is that if we are walking according to the call and abilities of the Lord, there is really no risk. Risk entails uncertainty. The Christian entrepreneur can go beyond uncertainty by knowing his calling in life and being constantly led by the Holy Spirit.

"... because those who are led by the Spirit of God are sons of God" (Romans 8:14).

As a child of God, you should be led by His Spirit. This is no less true concerning your business. Each day and every step of the way you must seek to be in communion with the Spirit in order to understand the steps He has determined for you. The greatest measure of success, prosperity and opportunity to be a powerful witness to those around you will come as you are led by the Spirit.

> *"Since we live by the Spirit, let us keep in step with the Spirit" (Galatians 5:25).*

The only way you can ever hope to keep pace with the demands and challenges of business is by keeping in step with the Spirit. As you do, you will see God's hand on everything you do and the miraculous will occur in your endeavors. When you are led by the Spirit, you will accomplish things you would not think possible.

> *"A man's steps are directed by the Lord. How then can anyone understand his own way?" (Proverbs 20:24)*

There will be uncertainties when you pursue a business undertaking with your own natural understanding and by your own wits. But you will reduce the risk factor and that sense of uncertainty when you:

> *"Trust in the Lord with all your heart and lean not on your own understanding; in all your ways acknowledge him, and he will make your paths straight" (Proverbs 3:5-6).*

One of the most debilitating attacks on any entrepreneur's life is anxiety.

276

"Do not be anxious about anything, but in everything, by prayer and petition, with thanksgiving, present your requests to God. And the peace of God, which transcends all understanding, will guard your hearts and your minds in Christ Jesus" (Philippians 4:6-7).

God never intended you to take on the pressures of risk usually associated with undertaking a business venture. As a Christian entrepreneur, you can eliminate anxiety and maintain the encouragement and peace so necessary for your success. This is possible through communion with your loving heavenly Father in prayer.

Unless you are called to be an entrepreneur, you may find starting and operating a business a bit agonizing over the long haul. You may also discover you are less than fully effective and satisfied in this role. If you are truly called and equipped, you will operate with a passion and not in desperation to make the enterprise everything it should be. With this passion, you will find the determination to stand when the going seems rough—when the enemy is taking shots at you. If you are called, properly equipped and solidly committed, you will out class and out power the enemy at every turn.

For The Sake of Profit:

Profit is not a dirty word. In fact, it should be obvious that no business can long survive without being profitable. While the only motivation indicated in Webster's definition of an entrepreneur is profit, for the Christian entrepreneur, this should never be the primary motivating factor.

"Do not wear yourself out to get rich; have the wisdom to show restraint. Cast but a glance at riches, and they are gone" (Proverbs 23:4-5).

Riches can be elusive and uncertain when you directly pursue them. As a Christian entrepreneur, operating according to the Word of God, you have a great advantage. You don't have to pursue riches, blessings will overtake you.

"Misfortune pursues the sinner, but prosperity is the reward of the righteous" (Proverbs 13:21).
"The blessing of the Lord brings wealth, and he adds no trouble to it" (Proverbs 10:22).
"Blessed is the man who finds wisdom, the man who gains understanding, for she is more profitable than silver and yields better returns than gold" (Proverbs 3:14-15).

Profit is the hope and desire of those operating a business in the world's system. Profit, wealth and prosperity are simply the by-product of the efforts and pursuits of the true Christian entrepreneur.

"For the pagans run after all these things, and your heavenly Father knows that you need them. But seek first his kingdom and his righteousness, and all these things will be given to you as well" (Matthew 6:32-33).

The world seeks riches. You will simply harvest riches by sowing to the Spirit. You sow to the Spirit by seeking God's will and purpose for you and applying godly principles in the pursuit of the business undertaking He has called you into.

What are the reasons you want to be in business for yourself? Is it being your own boss? Improving your standard of living? Freedom from the ourtine of a regular schedule? Whatever the other reasons are, you must first know beyond a doubt that this is what God has for you to do. Not everybody is called and gifted for this undertaking. There is a vast difference between what a man can do and what God—through a called and equipped man—can do.

Running a business is nothing like working for someone else. You are responsible for everything. Truly, the buck stops with you. Are you a self-starter, capable of planning, organizing and carrying out projects on your own initiative? If not, you may find starting and running a business a miserable existence. If this all still sounds good to you, you may just be called to operate your own business. It can be a source of immense satisfaction and can provide many wonderful rewards.

You are an entrepreneur—but now what? Discover the important role you are to play in the business arena before the window of opportunity closes!

Personal
Growth

The Order of Business

Pat Robertson

THE ORDER OF BUSINESS

Pat Robertson dreamed of making it big in business, then giving of his wealth to those in need. It turns out, he had the order reversed—he had to first give out of his need before business could succeed.

by Brian Mast

Life is full of paradoxes. For Pat Robertson, an honor grad from military prep school, Golden Gloves boxer, Marine combat officer in Korea with a law degree from Yale, and the son of a US Senator, life seemed empty and futile.

"What is the matter with me?" Pat kept asking himself. It was 1956 and Pat was in the electronic component business with a few of his old law school buddies. Business was good and he and his wife Dede were enjoying the high life of New York, but everything still seemed empty.

His mother's long letters were no help, as she regularly said, "Pat, God has a plan for your life and you will never be happy until you are in the center of that plan." Pat and Dede didn't have time for his "religious fanatic" mother, so they tossed her unopened letters aside. But Pat couldn't shake the feeling that maybe God was calling him.

One night he prayed, "All right, God, let me make my fortune, then I'll become a philanthropist and give all my money away for the good of mankind." He admits, "I had a hunch God wasn't pleased with my offer. Inside, I knew God would never be satisfied until I gave him my all, but I didn't understand how the 'all' part worked."

Several months later, as a dinner guest at an expensive restaurant, Pat found the answer he had been seeking. "You may have accepted God," said the elderly missionary who sat across the table from him, "but you haven't surrendered your life to Jesus." The truth of the aptly spoken words penetrated Pat's heart. "It was like a light went on in my head," he says. From that point on, life was different.

Pat began to have an increasing desire to be in ministry. He was able to sell his portion of the business and felt the next move would be to attend seminary. Though Pat and Dede learned and grew together in their faith, by the time his studies were completed, their income had dwindled to almost nothing. After a combined total of 10 years of further education, from law to engineering to theology, Pat still felt he lacked vision and purpose.

"I was willing to do anything that God showed me," Pat says, but nothing seemed to be happening. Dede had gone back home to Columbus, Ohio, to help her brother recover from surgery and Pat stayed home to pray for guidance. While praying, he felt he should read Luke 12:33, which said, "Sell all that ye have, and give alms..." So Pat wrote Dede, telling her briefly that God had spoken to him through Luke 12:33. Without reading the verse, she wrote back and said to do whatever he felt the Lord telling him to do.

A few days later, when she called from Ohio to see how Pat was doing, she found he had sold everything except the baby bed, a few wedding presents, her clothes, their old car, and a few pots and pans. And the money gained from their prized furniture and other belongings Pat had given to an orphanage in Korea and to a homeless family in Brooklyn. Needless to say, Dede was highly irritated.

When he picked her up a few days later on their way to visit his parents in Lexington, Virginia, she was still upset, but Pat felt strangely confident that he had made the correct decision. They arrived in town on a Friday night and on Monday morning his mother handed him a letter she had received in the mail. An old classmate he hadn't seen in 16 years had written Pat's mother, then added a casual PS that read: "There is a television station in Portsmouth, Virginia, that has gone defunct and is on the market. Would Pat be interested in claiming it for the Lord?"

Something even greater than Pat had planned or imagined was beginning to take place. Two days later, while sitting at a red light, Pat looked up and saw the very man who had written the unusual letter. Pat leapt out of his car and said, "George Lauderdale, what are you doing here?"

Lauderdale had driven the 240 miles to Lexington that very morning because he felt he needed to, and now he knew why. Over a cup of coffee at a corner drugstore, Pat probed for more information about the station. The UHF station was off the air, he discovered, and to build a similar one would cost between $250,000 and $300,000.

"Where could I get that kind of money?" Pat blurted out.

"It will sell for much less than that," Lauderdale said. "Besides, the Lord can supply the need."

Later that evening, with Lauderdale's words still ringing in his ears, Pat went outside to pray. He looked up at the night sky and said, "Lord, if you want me to buy the station, you are going to have to tell me how much to pay, because I don't know anything about television."

Immediately, an amount came to mind—$37,000.

Very small beginnings

The price might as well have been $37 million, Dede was quick to point out, and though Pat agreed, he knew he had to take the next step and begin negotiations. Pat wrote the owner asking how much he wanted for the station, and received back a quick response. The asking price was $75,000: $25,000 for the equipment and $50,000 for the land and building.

With no resources and no clear direction, they returned to their small quarters in New York. Three difficult months later, in early November of 1959, Pat felt it was time to purchase the TV station-sight unseen.

Pat and Dede and their three children loaded all their possessions into a 5 x 7 U-Haul trailer behind their stationwagon and left New York for Portsmouth, Virginia. Though Pat only had $70 dollars to his name, he was happy to be on his way.

The $70 went quickly. Dede was able to get a part-time job as a nurse at a local hospital and Pat was asked to preach regularly in a local church. Their own bills were scarcely met, and they were in no position to begin any form of financial negotiation.

The TV station, it turned out, had been vandalized and left vacant for quite some time. When Pat finally tracked down the owner, the offering price of $37,000 was met with a laugh. He was, however, willing to negotiate.

After much prayer from Pat and Dede's part, and several "unexplainable" concessions from the owner, the station, along with the land and building, were sold to Pat for $37,000.

The Christian Broadcasting Network, Inc. (CBN) was officially in existence on January 11, 1960, but the station had months of cleanup yet to do, the broadcasting license needed to be reinstated, pre-existing loans were due, staff needed to be hired, and funds were in very short supply. The first big step had been taken, but the task that lay ahead seemed monstrous. Almost two years after Pat arrived in the Portsmouth area, CBN made it on the air for the first time on October 1, 1961.

During CBN's formative years, desperate moments and unexpected provisions were commonplace. At one point a wealthy businessman offered to give CBN a large sum of money, enough to cover all the costs, but the deal fell through. Pat was disappointed, but Dede's words struck home. "God wants this station run on prayer, and nickel and dime support. If you had received that big sum, it would have shut off the prayer and financial support you need so badly from the thousands of people in this area. Remember Pat, we're supposed to be walking by faith and not by sight. Always."

It was around that time that Pat struck bottom and decided to sell the station. Everything and everyone seemed to be turning against him. Local pastors would have nothing to do with him, financial support had dwindled away to almost nothing, some of the staff had left, and $10,000 was due RCA. "If something didn't happen soon," Pat said, "we will be in the absurd position of having a 'faith' ministry file bankruptcy."

A few days later he drove to Washington, DC, and approached his Board of Directors with his decision, but the advice he received was not what he expected. They not only encouraged him to continue, but they refused to sell their part of the corporation and proceeded to tell Pat that he was proud and that God was using the circumstances to humble him. "They were being brutal," Pat says, "but my spirit agreed with every word. These were the wounds of a friend."

The next day at a gathering of Christian businessmen, Pat felt as if God said to him, "This is my work. I'll carry the burden." From that moment on, the weight he felt around his neck was gone, replaced by faith.

Immediately after the meeting, Pat received a telegram from an unknown individual that said, in essence, "Don't sell the station. I am immediately pledging $500 toward your work and will do all I can to help you." Though the circumstances hadn't changed, Pat returned home a different man.

Breakthrough—Inch by Inch

"In those early days we had no real concept of how to minister on television," Pat says. "It was as if God wanted us to start small and build, for it took time and struggle to learn what God really wanted us to do."

Little by little, the pieces began to come together. Qualified staff began to trickle in, financial support began to come in for Pat and the community began to get involved by praying, volunteering, and giving. The little radio station that they had acquired but tried to get rid of ended up back in their hands. Later, it would turn out, the little radio station, outfitted with a new transmitter, would overnight quadruple CBN's audience. The increased coverage meant increased prayer and financial support.

In 1963, CBN's budget had increased to $7000-a-month, but the giving was far short of the needed amount. Pat knew quitting the ministry was not an option, and similarly he felt that selling commercials to raise capital was not right. Since CBN and the staff were living by faith, he reasoned that it was time to ask the listening and viewing audiences to do the same.

CBN went on the air that fall asking 700 individuals to trust God for $10 each per month, enough to cover the monthly budget. Not all the needed funds were raised, but the first telethon, named The 700 Club, was such a success that they decided to run the telethon every year. Throughout the years, thousands of people have made a decision to follow Christ, while thousands of others have been healed while calling in and talking with prayer counselors. Though the show's format has changed over the years, The 700 Club is today one of the longest running daily programs in television history.

As opportunities increased to reach the local community and beyond, so did the need for a larger budget. A radio station in Bogota, Columbia, strong enough to reach beyond the city's 2.5 million inhabitants, was for sale, and donations poured in, providing CBN with its first radio station in South America. Then, in New York five radio stations were miraculously given to CBN as a tax write-off, valued at $600,000 dollars. By January 1, 1969, CBN's television and radio stations were reaching over 10 million people, twenty-four hours a day. The doors were opening one after another

In 1970, a gift of $300 million, what seemed to be an answer to prayer, turned out to be a dead end trail.

When the deal fell through, Pat was again forced to recognize that not only was God in control, but that all Pat had to do was focus on his original calling: to minister to the "little guys" in need. If he was faithful to do that, the finances would be sure to come in. And they did.

The Next Level

By 1973, CBN was bursting at the seams, and when the Board of Directors decided to give a tenth of all CBN's income to other Christ-focused ministries, the growth became exponential (1974 tripled the results of 1973, and 1975 doubled 1974!). Through television alone, CBN was now reaching 100 million viewers through its 40 television and radio stations across the US and several other stations in Canada and overseas.

When 142 acres went on the market in nearby Virginia Beach, Pat thought he heard a voice simply say, "Buy the entire tract of land and build a headquarters and a school for my glory!" Despite the fact that cash was in short supply, he went ahead with the purchase, and financial support began to arrive. Construction started soon after on a satellite station that would effectively link CBN's programming to the nations of the world. Next came the School of Communication, the first part of what is now Regent University, a fully accredited graduate school. Construction on the property, and an additional 540 acres purchased at a later date, continued as the funds became available.

By 1981, CBN was reaching 10 million homes. The cable network part of the ministry was sold in 1990 to International Family Entertainment, Inc. (IFE), a publicly held company Pat founded that traded on the New York Stock Exchange. IFE, which included the old Family Channel, the old MTM Productions, an English Family

Channel, and several other small cable efforts, was then sold in 1997 to Fox Kids Worldwide, Inc. for $1.9 billion dollars.

When asked about the sale to a "secular" company, Pat explains, "We sold IFE for $1.9 billion dollars, which is an astounding price. It was the thing that was needed to fund our international evangelism outreach for the Gospel." Of the proceeds from the sale, approximately $136 million went to the ongoing ministry of CBN, with an additional $110 million placed in a charitable trust that will be transferred to CBN in 2010. In addition, Regent received almost $150 million from stock sales, and when coupled with previous investments, the total endowment of more than $275 million makes Regent University the best endowed university in Christian education.

"All we gave up was access to make major TV movies, and the ability to buy other shows," Pat points out. "And we were able to maintain what we wanted, and that was keeping access to a cable network in perpetuity." The 17.5 hours a week of air time that CBN retained to broadcast The 700 Club is worth a minimum of $250 million dollars. The bottom line in the sale, Pat is pleased to say, "is that CBN was a major beneficiary of the whole transaction."

The success of Pat and CBN, in both the ministry and the business sense, was no accident. Every plan and vision, he has come to recognize, is secondary to obeying the voice of God. After all, following the proper order is everything.

Much of the biographical information is from CBN's 25th Anniversary edition of Shout it from the Housetops, by Pat Robertson with Jamie Buckingham. Used with permission.

GET A LIFE!

by Jeff Conley

If work dominates your world, it may be time to do a little soul searching...and find the habits of your heart.

Are you so over-worked that every day at 3 p.m. you secretly desire to go home and become one with your sofa? Every profession has "seasons of intensity"—accountants with tax deadlines, attorneys in the middle of a big case and sales people at the end of the month. During these seasons of intensity, we tend to adapt to the demands of our jobs and exceed expectations. No problem, at least not yet.

Hard work is a virtue, but constant overwork is a liability. While seasons of intensity and occasional sacrifices are justifiable in the short-term, a work culture that demands constant sacrifice of time away from family is toxic to the long-term success of both the enterprise and the individual. Constant intensity starves the spirit and cancels the creativity and passion that led you to your profession.

If you are currently working under a model of results that believes the only path to success is through sixty to seventy hours a week at work and broken promises to yourself and your family, you need to know there are other paths. There are paths to success wide enough for family, friends and fun. The key is in the ability to recognize these paths and the having the desire to take them.

How do you know if you are working on the wrong path? When you see one of life's biggest red flags that says, "When your work becomes the dominating force adversely affecting your family, it's time to make a change—a change in attitude or a change in the way you work."

Change—or Else!

The story of Roy Neel illustrates the concept of changing the way we work to help build a path for lasting and complete success. Roy's story appeared in the March 6, 1995 issue of Newsweek, which described him as the deputy chief of staff in the Clinton administration. Roy's days were full, he worked fifty-five hours each week, and he was always on call:

I got downright tired of being tethered to my beeper 24 hours a day," says Neel. A seemingly tame but wrenching episode with Walter, his nine-year-old son, convinced him that work, even for the President of the United States, was not worth the price. Walter and his dad were heading out the door for a long-promised baseball game when the phone rang. It was the President. Little Walter was not impressed. When Neel looked up an hour later, Walter was gone. He had bummed a ride with a neighbor, leaving dad holding the phone. "Our society is schizophrenic," says Neel. "We praise people who want to balance their lives, but reward those who work themselves to death."

Neel listened to his wake-up call. He saw life's big red flag and found a new path to success, one that was wide enough to take Walter and the rest of his family along for the ride. How about you? Are you ready to find your new path?

For ten years I've wrestled with finding a simpler but successful path at work and being the kind of parent and spouse my family deserves. I have found a way to do both. My discovery happened when I started asking myself some soul-searching questions. I wrote them down in my day planner, only to find that they haunted me daily.

These questions were important because they challenged me to find an invariable sense of direction in times of confusion and constant change. They helped me feel that I was part of something that was bigger than myself.

I began condensing my list of short bite-sized questions related to finding the path to success that would fit my dreams and my family. I named these bite-sized questions "Habits of the Heart." Each Habit of the Heart was meant to be a gentle reminder of the feedings necessary to nourish the hungers of the heart. Ask yourself these 13 questions every day:

1. Am I sure about what matters most?
2. Did I make a difference today?
3. Am I secure in who I am regardless of my performance?
4. Did I schedule some quiet time today?
5. What did I do to show my family that I love them?
6. Did I keep all my commitments (especially those at home?)
7. Did I protect my honesty and integrity?

8.   Did I read or learn anything new?
9.   Did I laugh out loud today?
10.   Was I a model of excellence at work today?
11.   If today was a day off, did I rest or was I restless?
12.   Did I provide emotional support for my family today?
13.   What will I do differently tomorrow?

The greatest discovery I've made is that if I were to be hit and killed by a big truck today, I'd be replaced at work tomorrow. But I'll never be replaced at home. I'd be missed there forever. Stop giving your family the leftovers of yourself. Use these questions to remind yourself that a wider path to success is out there, one that is wide enough for family, friends and fun.

Jeff Conley is a committed husband and father who also happens to have been named by Speakers Platform as one of the world's top ten motivational speakers. At work, Jeff is CEO of Jeff Conley Corporation, a business resource that helps business people build closer relationships with their customers, co-workers and families. He has authored: Habits of the Heart: Taking Paths to Success Wide Enough For Family, Friends and Fun. Mr. Conley can be reached at (972) 242-4300 or emailed at Conleycorp@aol.com

THE BENEFITS OF STRESS

by Edwin Louis Cole

Living a stress free life may not be what you need—or want

Stress at almost intolerable levels is being experienced in every segment of life in every nation on earth. U.S. business is on the move, with a half million firms relocating to new facilities in 1989. Upheavals accompany such moves, with two-thirds of executives fired, demoted, or quitting.[1]

Office stress follows many home. Reports say 28 percent of all managers bring stress home, but 57 percent say they rarely bring family tensions to work.[2] At the same time, studies indicate that stress in the home is often greater than stress at work. Unemployment among men produced the highest levels of stress in every survey. Work problems and related financial difficulties are a central theme not only in male suicides, but also in suicide-homicide cases. Many men use work to avoid dealing with personal problems. Men work longer hours when they are facing problems, the idea being that if you keep busy, you don't have to feel. I'm not saying any of this is right or wrong, just that it's there.

Stress

Financial stress is universally felt. Debtor nations are at the mercy of others, while those who loan are beholden to prop up the failing economies of those who borrow.

Personal debt on the individual level kills the productivity through which nations become strong. Easy credit allures. High interest credit cards are proliferating among unemployed college students in America. College presidents are using their time to battle the crisis created by greed.

Some young married couples are encouraged by salesmen, marketers, advertisers, and bankers to have all they want through easy payment plans, only to be trapped by usury. Seduced by avarice, they try to accumulate in three years of marriage what it took their parents thirty years to obtain. Debt puts a strain on the relationship that often fractures it. Some recognize temptation for what it is and others don't.

Financial pressure, like any stress, can drive men to desperation, but needn't overwhelm the real man. A friend of mine telephoned me to say, "In two more months I'll be completely out of debt."

"I'm thrilled for you," I replied. "How much did you owe?"

"Five million dollars," he said, "and now after two years I'm going to be debt free. It was a struggle but we made it."

Bankers had loaned him money to pay the interest on money he had borrowed, snowballing until his debt finally totaled five million dollars. A successful real estate developer, he now saw very little of his money. Almost all was going to banks. The pressure was intense. Then one night in prayer, he sought God's strategy through wisdom from the Word, and God dropped a gift of faith in his heart. As he believed by faith that God would see him through, he scribbled out new terms for handling the debt. The next day he put a halt to the cycle by telling the bankers he wasn't playing their game anymore, and laid down the new terms God had helped him formulate. The bankers fumed and fussed, but agreed. Now after only two years he was totally out of debt.

In—but not under—Stress

Jesus was without personal stress in Himself, though He bore the sins of the world. Admitting that He was only doing what He saw the Father do relieved Him from the pressure of having to perform on His own. He had the backing of heaven for all He did (John 5:19-20).

He never manipulated, threatened, or gave ultimatums. He spoke "as one having authority, and not as the scribes" (Matthew 7:29). His authority came in part from His knowledge of Who he was, His purpose in life, and an identity with which He was in perfect agreement.

Real men are Christlike. Identified with Jesus, secure in that identity, acting in faith on God's Word, believing God will perform what He says, they move through life's trials and circumstances with confidence, and face adversity with courage.

Pressure is normal and even needed in life. The right amount of tension in a guitar or piano string is necessary for fine tuning. Too much and it will snap. Carbon, graphite, and diamonds are made from the same substance—it's the pressure that makes the difference. The more pressure matter is able to withstand, the more valuable it becomes. It's the same with people.

A pastor and friend of mine in Florida was undergoing pressure that seemed unbearable. A godly man, desiring to do the right thing in the midst of much wrong, he had to struggle to maintain his personal equilibrium, to minister in love and grace, and to determine the will of God for his life and congregation.

During that time he found some positive aspects of stress in his life:

Stress is necessary for spiritual growth (James 1:2-4)
Stress produces more love in committed people (Romans 5:3-5)

Stress produces a greater degree of sanctification (1 Peter 1:6-7)

Testing prepares you for greater works (Revelation 3:12)

Stress causes the greatest need for prayer (Philippians 4:6)

Stress comes from resisting Satan (1 Peter 5:9)

Testing comes before victory (James 1:12; Romans 8:35-37)

Stress produces seeking after God, and that glorifies Him (1 Peter 4:12-13)

Stress is not a new phenomenon in life. The greater the responsibility, the greater the pressure. All trials and temptations will end positively if we remain committed to God. God always starts on the positive and ends on the positive. It is the nature of God to change things in our lives for the good. There is pressure in change, but change is the only constant in maturity.

All that is stressful in your life today has the potential for good or for harm. Determine to be changed through the refining fire of pressure, believe God to enable you to overcome the fivefold temptations, lose yourself in identity with Jesus Christ, seek His wisdom in the particularly critical decisions, and let stress work for the good to make you a stronger man.

[1]) "Research Recommendations," issued by National Institute of Business Management, 6 March 1989, 2.

[2]) Fred Williams, "Office Stress Follows Many Home," USA Today, 15 March 1990, 8B, citing survey by Dunhill Personnel System, Inc.

Chick-fil-A
Truett's Way

S. Truett Cathy

Truett's Way

The name may ring a bell, or it may simply make you salivate, but Truett Cathy has made Chick-fil-A more than just a tasty sandwich.

by Brian Mast

The marketplace is teeming with "successful" leaders and businessmen who are more than willing to sell their "how to" advice on getting rich. Success, however, is about more than simply making money and businessmen everywhere are searching for a sound example to follow. Realizing that they will inevitably retain the characteristics of the individual they most admire, many are careful in their selection. The best example to follow is a man who has truly succeeded in every aspect of life.

Meet S. Truett Cathy, the unassuming founder, chairman and Chief Executive Officer of fast food giant Chick-fil-A. Few would question this man's success. With 735 locations in malls, airports, hospitals, universities, supermarkets, and free-standing units, Chick-fil-A is an ever expanding force in the quick-service restaurant arena. Cathy has been the recipient of countless awards over the years, including the prestigious Horatio Alger Award in 1989. Although a true success story who is now able to enjoy the bountiful fruits of his perseverance and hard work, Truett Cathy is quick to recall the old days when he was alone and insignificant in the restaurant world.

Humble Beginnings

In 1946, Truett Cathy and his brother Ben opened a small diner in Hapeville, Georgia, an Atlanta suburb. They pulled triple shifts and simply wore every hat required, be it cleaning, cooking, marketing, advertising, or waiting tables. Cathy always worked hard and hoped that one day his efforts and principles would pay off, and they did.

Cathy and his brother started their restaurant venture with very little money (a $6,600 loan from a local bank and $4,000 cash from, among other sources, the sale of Cathy's car) and a surplus amount of grit and determination. From the beginning they were faced with difficulties, and Cathy says now that if he had known how difficult it would turn out to be, he probably would not have gotten into the restaurant business. But hindsight is "20/20" and he had no such revelation. His motto, "Every problem has a solution," proved to be the principle upon which he founded and operated his business.

From Truett Cathy's Point of View...
Success

According to Truett Cathy, success cannot be measured in monetary units. Of course, making a profit is desired and expected, but it is not the sole aim of his company. Success for him is time with his family, watching those he helped influence become what they only dreamed they could be, and investing time and money into foster children or others who need it. In fact, immediately following this interview, he was heading to one of his 10 foster homes. He said that he makes the children pop-corn and hot chocolate and rocks them to sleep, something that most of the children have never experienced.

Being successful, according to Cathy, also means maintaining Godly principles without waivering. For Cathy, being closed on Sundays is a decision that he will not revoke, regardless of the cost. This has meant losing restaurant sites and not receiving some prime locations in malls, but Cathy doesn't mind. Sundays were always special for him as a child, since he had the day off from school and work and could go to church. He wants his employees to be able to enjoy a day of rest and not be pressured to work. Remarkably, Chick-fil-A often out-performs other restaurants in six days anyway. For Cathy, the financial success of his business is simply the result of his actions rather than the goal of his life.

Life

His goals were much the same as every young businessman's, but he quickly learned the importance of balance. At times he was forced to work 36 hour shifts when he and his brother were just beginning and the restaurant demanded their time, but he was unwilling to compromise on his beliefs. This unwavering attitude helped keep his priorities in balance. His relationship with God, his wife, and his family were constantly on the top of his priority list. At times, admittedly, his work schedule interfered with priorities, but he was quick to change it as soon as he could.

The desire to walk in balance preempted his business decisions. Instead of jumping ahead when situations looked great, he would prepare himself first. After seeing a man fall to his death while mountain climbing, Cathy has always walked cautuiously, yet steadily, in his business. Because his personal and family life was in order, he could devote more attention to work when it was appropriate without fearing a family crisis.

He has continually emerged the victor, despite the challenge.

Difficulties and Impossibilities

Building the first restaurant, called the Dwarf Grill (later renamed the Dwarf House), turned out to be more complicated than Cathy and his brother Ben had anticipated. World War II efforts had reduced the amount of construction materials and food goods available to the public. Larger businesses had already secured the building supplies and more established restaurants controlled the food market. Cathy and his brother were forced to salvage wood and nails while working on their own restaurant to meet the opening deadline. Meat, oil, sugar, flour, and other basic ingredients were in short supply as well, so Cathy asked a larger restaurant owner to order extra and then sell it to them. The ploy worked and the Cathys were officially in the restaurant business. Despite the odds, they opened on schedule and made a profit from the very start.

As their business boomed, they found they were not able to buy enough beef to satisfy the demand. Cathy labored over this predicament for a long time, and then had an idea. He approached the cattle farmers directly and worked out a deal that allowed him to buy all the meat he needed for the restaurant. It worked, and they were back in business.

Cathy did face other obstacles, even more difficult than the construction of the first Dwarf House, but his determination and faith in God gave him the drive and peace to continue. In 1949, just three years after opening the first restaurant, Cathy's brother and partner, Ben, died in a plane crash. His only other brother, Horace, and

310

two other men, also died in the accident. Then, in 1960, the second Dwarf House burned to the ground. That same year he had to undergo two surgeries to remove polyps from his colon. He had expected to die in the hospital, but his wife Jeannette told him, "Truett, God isn't finished with your life yet and I don't think He's going to take you." Cathy recovered and soon regained his fervor for living. In all the challenges and trials, he has never lost perspective of his role in life. He believes that God does have a plan for him and he intends to accomplish it, no matter the cost.

Management

Cathy has taken seriously the role of employer and has deposited, quite literally, into the lives of his employees. He has given over $12 million in scholarships to promising restaurant employees with the goal of helping those who work for him accomplish what they desire and want in life.

When Cathy found out one of his employees had dropped out of school to help support his family, he spoke with the young man's father and worked out a compromise so that the boy could work part-time and continue to go to school. In the end, the young man became a school teacher and later an award-winning school principal. Cathy is careful with those he hires and invests time and effort into the lives of his employees. The result: Chick-fil-A has one of the lowest turnover rates in the restaurant industry, both in management (operators) and part-time positions.

Customer Comments and Quality

Cathy prides himself in listening to his customer's comments. In fact, while developing the Chick-fil-A

Chicken Sandwiches, over 36 years ago, he experimented with different spices and asked his customers what they thought. When they stopped making comments, he concluded that he had the perfect taste, and he stuck with it. Today he says with a smile, "My customers were the ones who helped me invent the recipe for what became the Chick-fil-A Chicken Sandwich." His customers always came back, and brought others with them.

The goal of each Chick-fil-A restaurant is to provide an attractive, clean, and pleasurable eating experience. With such intentions, it is no wonder that sales have increased steadily over the past 30 years. As the chain has increased, so has the commitment to offer a better product and service than other fast-food restaurants. Chick-fil-A management believes that the chain must get better before it gets bigger.

Accountability

In 1982, Chick-fil-A experienced a serious financial downturn, and Truett Cathy took it personally. He asked God to show him what he had done wrong and pledged he would do whatever it took to change the situation. He refused a salary that year so others wouldn't have to take a cut in pay. He then asked his wife and executive staff for help. Cathy not only recognized the primary importance of being right with God, but he also sought the wise counsel available to him from his wife and other staff members.

Later that year they held an executive committee meeting away from the office and distractions where together they discussed possible solutions to the financial crisis. The result was the formation of Chick-fil-A's Corporate Purpose Statement which brought renewed focus on being a positive Christian witness to the public, moving more aggressively, and challenging the competition. Within six months Chick-fil-A rebounded with a more than 40% increase in sales (A bronze plaque with the corporate purpose statement now stands at the front entrance of the company's headquarters in Atlanta. Bought as a gift for Cathy by his employees, it has special meaning.)

Regardless of the "natural" reason for advancement and increased revenue, Cathy is always quick to give credit and thanks to God. The day he opened his first restaurant in 1946 was monumental in his career, and that night he walked outside and thanked God for helping them and for giving them "the courage to start and to keep going" (It's Easier to Succeed than to Fail, 1989). Because he maintained perspective, he knew who really deserved credit for his achievements, and as a result, God blessed him even more. Now, 53 years later, nobody can deny God's hand of blessing on Truett Cathy.

A Word to the Wise ...

Truett Cathy's life is not a "how to" approach on making it rich, but rather a testimony of one man's walk with God and how following godly principles resulted in tremendous blessings. Following Cathy's example will benefit any business, but obeying Christ is the only guarantee of true success in every area of life

Being a Real Christian

Though Cathy won't hesitate to explain the importance of Jesus Christ in his life, he does not require others working for him to believe like him. He does, however, expect incorporation of Biblical principles into the operation. Treating employees and customers with respect, being honest and clean, closing on Sundays, and continually trying to provide an enjoyable eating environment, are policies that are expected from everyone at Chick-fil-A. Cathy's example often speaks louder than words, and he likes it that way.

He has overcome enough obstacles in his restaurant business to realize that being a Christian doesn't make him immune to difficulties, but he knows that God is in control and that he has a part to play in the business world today. HisChristian witness is evident and proclaimed by everyone in the business community. Truett Cathy is indeed letting his light shine before all men.

Retirement

For Cathy, fifty-three years is a long time to be in the same business, much less the same restaurant (His 50-plus years in the restaurant business give Cathy the distinction of being Atlanta's restauranteur with the most years of continuous service.), but he shows no sign of tiring. He still spends ample time at the restaurants, works in his office, and visits the children of several foster homes. In addition, he finds time to teach Sunday school to 13-year-old boys at his local church, something he has been doing for the past 42 years.

As for retirement, that is a word Cathy seems to have never learned. Jeannette, Cathy's wife of 51 years, understands his zeal for life and knows better than to expect him to come home any time soon. Even when Cathy does turn more control of Chick-fil-A over to his sons, Dan and "Bubba"(Donald), he will continue to have a role to play in the business. Nevertheless, he is confident that his sons will maintain the same godly principles that he has upheld over the last fifty-two years. Dan, currently the Executive Vice-President and President of Chick-fil-A International, and Bubba, Senior Vice-President and President of the Dwarf House, are ready to lead Chick-fil-A into the next generation. Until then, the challenges and excitement of business continue to move Cathy, and he will keep working as long as God grants him breath.

Don't Let Things Stick To You

by John Mason

We can be free from the failures and mistakes of the past—free to accomplish things for the future.

As I have had the privilege of meeting hundreds of people over the past several years, one thing that always stands out to me is how many people have things attached to them. For example, people allow a critical statement made by a third-grade teacher, a failure or mistake made ten or fifteen years ago or the comments of a negative neighbor last week hold them back from their destiny. It is a foolish man that adheres to all that he hears. Not everyone has a right to speak into your life. Not every word requires an answer. One of the most powerful principles that you can apply to acquire momentum is the principle of not letting things stick to you.

I really believe that one of the major benefits of asking forgiveness from God is that things no longer "stick to us." He says that if we confess our sins He is faithful and just to forgive us of our sins. But incredibly, God doesn't stop there (and that would be great enough), but He also promises to cleanse us from all unrighteousness (See 2 Pet. 2:13). When He cleanses us

317

from all unrighteousness, He gives us a right standing before the Father. Why? He doesn't want things to stick to us. When we have received a right standing before the Father, we are free of the failures and mistakes, wrong words and attitudes of the past, and we are released and free to accomplish things for the future.

Don't worry if you don't get what you think you should. What seems so necessary today might not even be desirable tomorrow.

Paul Harvey was right when he said, "In times like these, it helps to recall that there have always been times like these." If we can forget our troubles as easily as we forget our blessings, how different things would be.

One way to be free of things that want to stick to you is to take your mind off the things that seem to be against you. Thinking about these negative factors simply builds into them a power that they truly don't possess. Talking about your grievances merely adds to those grievances.

Attach yourself to God's forgiveness, plan and Word. Then watch yourself become loosed from former "sticky" situations.

Be The First To Forgive

Living a life of unforgiveness is like leaving the parking brake on when you drive your car. It causes you to slow down and lose your momentum. One of the most expensive luxuries that you can possess is unforgiveness toward someone. A deep-seated grudge in your life eats away at your peace of mind like a deadly cancer, destroying a vital organ of life. In fact, there are few things as pathetic and terrible to behold as the person who has harbored a grudge and hatred for many years.

The heaviest load that you can possibly carry on your back is a pack of grudges. So if you want to travel far and fast, then travel light. Unpack all of your envies, jealousies, grievances, revenges and fears.

Never reject forgiveness or the opportunity to forgive. The weak can never forgive because forgiveness is a characteristic of the strong. When you live a life of unforgiveness, revenge naturally follows. But revenge is the deceiver. It looks sweet, but it's most often bitter. It always cost more to avenge a wrong than to bear it. You never can win by trying to even the score.

Be the first to forgive. Forgiveness can be your deepest need and highest achievement. Without forgiveness, life is governed by an endless cycle of resentment and retaliation. What a dreadful waste of effort. "He who has not forgiven an enemy has never yet tasted one of the most sublime enjoyments of life," declares Johann Lavater.

Forgiving those who have wronged you is a key to personal peace. What the world needs is that peace that passes all misunderstanding. Forgiveness releases you for action and freedom.

Never cut what can be untied. Don't burn bridges. You'll be surprised how many times you have to cross over that same river. Unforgiveness is empty, but forgiveness makes a future possible. You'll "start your day on the right foot" if you ask yourself everyday, "Who do I need to forgive?"

Momentum Makers

1.   Choice   2. Commitment
3.   Dreams   4. Faith
5.   Prayer   6. Action
7.   Focus   8. Small Steps
9.   Listening   10. Creativity
11. Standing Alone   12. Wisdom
13. Zeal   14. Purpose
15. Positioning   16. Talents
17. The Word   18. Right Friends
19. Change   20. Forgiveness

Significance
Over Success

William Armstrong

SIGNIFICANCE OVER SUCCESS

The saying goes, a man of success achieves his goals, while a man of significance changes his world. William Armstrong is one who clearly understands the difference.

by Robert J. Tamasy

By any standard of business measurement, William Armstrong has proved to be successful. Consider the following:

He has served two six-year terms as a U.S. Senator from Colorado, earning the respect of colleagues in both parties. Early in 1988 he was mentioned as a serious candidate for the Presidency before then-Vice President George Bush chose to seek the nation's top office. Previously, Armstrong served six years as a congressman on Capitol Hill and 10 years in the Colorado state legislature.

An energetic entrepreneur, his first real job after high school was with a radio company in Omaha, Nebraska, before moving on to stations in New Orleans, Minneapolis and St. Louis. At the age of 21, starting on a thin financial shoestring, Armstrong bought his first radio station in Denver, and remained in the industry for more than 30 years. His interest in the broadcast media also led him into TV for 14 years, at one point owning three stations in Idaho and Wyoming before selling them in 1995.

At present he serves as the chairman of eight private companies, including mortgage banking, real estate, title insurance, and a general insurance agency, and is a director of three publicly held companies.

An articulate, effective communicator, Armstrong is in demand to speak all around the country, addressing large groups of business people 15-20 times a year.

He devotes considerable time to a variety of charitable and community non-profit organizations, and still works actively behind the scenes to support political candidates and causes.

In fulfilling his business responsibilities, charitable involvements and speaking engagements, Armstrong stockpiles frequent flyer miles by spending an average of 75 days on the road each year.

Significance over Success

Despite this impressive sum, of accomplishments, the pursuit of significance, not success, propels this 61-year-old former statesman. Today, his investments of time, energy and resources are directed toward endeavors that truly will change his world, particularly from an eternal perspective.

When Armstrong speaks, for example, his topic typically is not business or politics, even though he is eminently qualified to speak on either. Instead, he talks to his audiences about why a personal relationship with God is the one greatest asset any business person can have. And like E.F. Hutton, when Bill Armstrong speaks, people listen.

"I'm a firm believer that God calls each of us to particular kinds of things," Armstrong states. "He never called me to be a medical missionary or to plant churches overseas, but I believe I'm one of many men He has called to be a business missionary. He has given me many chances to show, and tell, what it means to be a Christian in the business world."

Related to that, each of the companies he chairs is intended to glorify God. Although all of the businesses have chief executive officers who oversee daily operations, he is very much involved in setting the overall philosophy and policy making.

"They are all secular organizations, but it's important that we conduct business on terms that honor the Lord. We're not trying to function like churches, but we want people, our employees and customers alike, to know where we stand in terms of values and beliefs."

His sense of calling as a "business missionary" has extended to his involvement in the Christian Business Men's Committee of USA, a lay ministry dedicated to evangelism and discipleship in the business and professional world. He also served on the board of directors of Campus Crusade for Christ International for seven years.

Through the Armstrong Family Foundation, established by his mother, Dorothy, Armstrong recently undertook two ambitious projects to communicate the gospel of Christ through the media in the Denver area.

He bought advertising space in the Denver Post, Rocky Mountain News, and Denver Business Journal to publish "Colorado Profiles," a series of features he commissioned to tell about the Christian commitment of well-known business and professional leaders in Colorado's Front Range. In one-minute radio spots, Armstrong had Christian friends tell seven different stories from the Bible that have clear application to life in modern America. Based on responses, both approaches were very effective in communicating biblical truth.

In terms of significance, however, Armstrong need not look any further than his own home. He and his wife, Ellen, have been married for 36 years. "Other than the decision to accept Christ," he points out, "who you marry is the most important decision you will ever make. It not only affects your personal happiness, but also how your children will turn out, and how the major themes of your life are played out."

Armstrong credits Ellen for keeping the family so close knit. They have two children, Wil and Anne, and seven grandchildren. Despite what some people say or think, Armstrong boldly states, "The most significant measure of a father or mother is whether or not their children really love Christ. Both of our children definitely do, and are teaching their children to do the same."

Wil is vice president of Cherry Creek Mortgage Company in Denver (one of the businesses his father chairs) and also serves as a director of Enterprise International, an agency that provides "micro-loans" to help needy people to get on their feet. According to the elder Armstrong, "This is one of the really smart things Christians are doing to help people, primarily overseas."

Anne, with her husband, Jamey Nordby, live in Black Forest, Colorado, where she homeschools three of their five sons. Armstrong is quick to note that "they both have an active, inspiring faith in the Lord Jesus," but it wasn't so long ago that Armstrong was far less interested in Jesus and accomplishing His will.

Success isn't Everything

Armstrong was introduced to a strong American work ethic by his parents while being raised in Fremont, Nebraska. It wasn't long before he discovered that the same principles worked well in striving for success. As a young adult, his goals were clear: establish a career in radio broadcasting, earn a million dollars before turning 30, acquire symbols of affluence, and become a member of a prominent country club.

Through natural business savvy and just plain hard work, most of his goals were attained within a several years. Next came urgings for him to seek public office.

Because of his strong opinions, people would tell him, "You keep talking about how things aren't going the way they ought to politically; maybe you should run for the state legislature." He did and was elected, first to the Colorado State House of Representatives and then to the State Senate.

After an unsuccessful race for Lieutenant Governor, Armstrong was ready to leave politics behind and return full-time to business and private life. But that year Colorado was awarded a fifth U.S. Congressional seat and he was persuaded to run.

Upon being elected, Armstrong was initially caught up in the excitement of being a U.S. representative and the electric atmosphere of Washington, D.C. After the adrenaline subsided, he discovered he was "one unhappy congressman." Power, prestige and position weren't nearly as fulfilling as expected, and he grew increasingly despondent.

"My early years in Congress were the worst of my life," he now explains. "I didn't have anything that made my life mean something. I didn't have answers to the age-old questions: What's my purpose? Why do I exist? Why am I here? Where am I going?"

One day a senior member of Congress gave Armstrong some advice that was appropriate, if not particularly helpful. He said, "Sonny, to achieve success in the U.S. House of Representatives, first of all you've got to learn humility."

If he had not felt so badly, Armstrong would have laughed. "I couldn't help but be humble. I was so unhappy. Everywhere I looked, I came up empty. Church didn't even have any meaning. It was something to do on Sunday morning, something good for the kids and a worthwhile organization to support financially, but it failed to provide me with the kind of organizing principle I needed for my life."

Then another friend approached him and showed him that the "organizing principle" he needed did not come from church, but from God.

Sitting in the Joe Martin dining room, a tiny room under the chamber of the House of Representatives, the friend showed Armstrong in a simple yet powerful way that the Lord had made full provision for the sense of purpose and meaning he longed for.

Armstrong remembers, "He told me that God loved me and had a wonderful plan for my life, but I was separated from God by sin. He explained this was true of every man, but that God had bridged the gap between me and Him by the death of Jesus Christ on the cross. It was up to me to make an individual decision to take advantage of what God had done for me that I could not do for myself."

"It was like a life preserver," Armstrong recalls of that moment in 1975. "If you are drowning, and someone throws you a life preserver, you can accept the fact that it can save your life, but it won't really do the job unless you actually grab hold of it."

He prayed that day, asking Jesus Christ to come into his life to forgive his sins and become his Savior and Lord. His life since has never been the same, as he explains, "I began to have an entirely new perspective on myself, and my new relationship with God started to greatly affect my other relationships, with my family, and with my colleagues on Capitol Hill."

His new faith did not prompt Armstrong to leave public office, but rather it provided a new sense of mission. He decided to run for the U.S. Senate in 1978, and when he was elected, began serving with strong optimism. He says, "I had a sense of total forgiveness, a feeling that I was not alone, and that it was not my responsibility to shoulder the burden of the world, or even my own life."

When he declined in 1990 to seek a third Senate term and left office early in 1991, Armstrong did so without regrets. "A U.S. senator has only three choices: He can keep running until he loses, he can continue winning and die in office, or he can voluntarily move on to other things. I simply chose the latter."

His decision was not an agonizing one, he notes, "because I never intended to be in Washington in the first place and certainly never planned to stay." He went back to where he felt he belonged, to the business world as a committed Christian, striving to demonstrate through both action and word that "Christian businessman" is not an oxymoron.

As far as vision and work are concerned, Armstrong has more than enough of both. But what keeps his attention are the countless individuals he comes in contact with who are in desperate need or the same "life preserver" he grabbed hold of several years ago.

Robert J. Tamasy is National Director of Publications for CBMC of USA, in Chattanooga, Tennessee. He is a co-author and editor of four books, including Jesus Works Here, published by Broadman & Holman Publishers.

THE SKY IS NOT THE LIMIT

by John Mason

No one can put a limit on you without your permission.

"Eli Whitney was laughed at when he showed his cotton gin. Edison had to install his electric light free of charge in an office building before anyone would even look at it. The first sewing machine was smashed to pieces by a Boston mob. People scoffed at the idea of railroads. People thought that traveling thirty miles an hour would stop the circulation of the blood. Morse had to plead before ten Congresses before they would even look at his telegraph," (Anonymous). Yet for all these men the sky was not the limit.

Beware of those who stand aloof and greet each venture with reproof; the world would stop if things were run by men who say, "It can't be done."

"Seek, and ye shall find" (Matt. 7:7). We attain only in proportion to what we attempt. More people are persuaded into believing in nothing than believing too much. Jesus said, "According to your faith be it unto you" (Matt. 9:29). You are never as far from the answer as it first appears. It's never safe or accurate to look into the future without faith.

Tell me what you believe about Jesus and I will tell you some important facts about your future. What picture of Jesus do you have? Is He merely a good man with good ideas? Or is He the Son of God, our advocate before God, the King of Kings and Lord of Lords?

A lot of people no longer hope for the best, they just hope to avoid the worst. Many of us have heard opportunity knocking at our door, but by the time we unhooked the chain, pushed back the bolt, turned two locks and shut off the burglar alarm—it was gone! Too many people spend their lives looking around, looking down or looking behind, when God says to look up. The sky's not the limit!

Not all obstacles are bad. In fact, an opportunity's favorite disguise is an obstacle. Conflict is simply meeting an obstacle on the road to your answer. The fight is good; it is proof that you haven't quit.

Growth and success don't eliminate obstacles; they create new ones. Thomas Carlisle said, "The block of granite which was an obstacle in the pathway of the weak becomes a stepping-stone in the pathway of the strong."

Trials provide an opportunity to grow, not die. Even in the midst of trials, God wants growth and promotion for you. Obstacles can temporarily detour you, but only you can make you stop. The devil wants you to think there's nothing more permanent than your temporary situation. Obstacles reveal what we truly believe and who we really are. They introduce you to yourself. Your struggle may be lasting, but it is not everlasting.

THE DIFFERENCE OF ONE

by Phil Downer

When an individual realizes his potential for influence, the world is never the same

In The Power of Vision, futurist Joel Barker recounts the story of a sage walking along a beach who was surprised to observe a young man running toward the water. He watched the man toss something into the sea, then run back across the sand, pick up something, and then sprint again toward the water and throw the object beyond the point where the waves were breaking.

"What are you doing?" the sage inquired.

"I'm saving starfish by throwing them back into the sea," the young man replied. "The sun is coming up and the tide is going out. If I don't act quickly, they all will die."

The sage chuckled at what he perceived as a futile effort. "But there are miles of beach, and many thousands of starfish lying on them right now. You can't possibly get to them all. What difference can you make?"

After listening politely, the young man bent over, picked up another starfish, ran toward the water and gently tossed it beyond the incoming waves. Turning to the sage, he answered, "I made a difference for that one."

This story is a vivid example for how God can use us as Christian businessmen. We may desire to be part of our Lord's Great Commission to "go therefore and make disciples" (Matthew 28:19), but the task seems almost hopeless. Years ago a census calculated there were about 20 million business and professional men in the United States. Today, that number is even greater. Most of them, as you and I know from personal experience, are not committed followers of Christ. How do we go about reaching so many unsaved businessmen with the gospel message? What difference can we make?

Like the young man with the helpless starfish, we too can make a difference—an eternal impact—even if God uses us in the life of only one man. When He touches the life of even a single person through you, more than one life is changed. The man's family is affected, as are people he works with, neighbors, friends, relatives and even strangers.

Playing a Vital Part

Terry and Jessica attended one of our CBMC conferences and for the first time caught the vision of "spiritual multiplication"—helping another person grow in his walk with Jesus Christ so he can help others.

Over the past seven years Terry and I have enjoyed spending time together, and I tried to help him understand how he, too, could have a life-changing impact. Terry and Jessica agreed to host Living Proof, a video training series on evangelism, in their home. However, the idea of becoming personally involved in evangelism and discipleship never quite clicked with Terry.

Then they attended a CBMC conference. They heard firsthand from other men and women how God touched their lives through other people, and how they are now investing their lives in others. Terry left that conference a different man.

He contacted a friend in Connecticut and convinced him he needed to be discipled by an older, godly man. The friend was enthusiastic, and Terry asked a CBMC staff member in Connecticut to follow up with him. Next, Terry called friends in Chicago and San Francisco, also urging them to be discipled by a seasoned man—both men agreed. Finally, Terry took steps to get involved himself by offering to disciple a friend in his city. The friend readily accepted, and Terry began to share from his own life to help another man grow, hoping one day that man will begin discipling another—and on and on. Like the young man on the beach, Terry wasn't worried about all the "starfish" beyond his reach; he knows it's enough just to try and help those he finds within his reach.

To his young pupil, the apostle Paul wrote, "And the things that you have heard from me in the presence of many witnesses, these entrust to faithful men who will be able to teach others also" (2 Timothy 2:2). In this one verse we see four generations of Christ's followers, and this principle still works very effectively today.

Several months ago my wife, Susy, and I were interviewed on a radio talk show. We explained how God, through a small group of faithful people, reached down and changed our lives, saved our marriage, and helped us gain a godly perspective about how to raise a family.

At the close of the program, we invited listeners to call our CBMC National Ministry Center in Chattanooga, Tennessee for more information or counseling.

One of the calls was particularly memorable. The young caller, very distraught, told about a horrible childhood she had endured. Her mother had gone so far as to say, "I wish I had aborted you and kept the other one!"

Thankfully, the woman was very open to hearing about the One whose love is limitless and unconditional, and Vickie, a member of our staff, was able over the phone to lead her in a prayer to receive Jesus Christ as her Savior and Lord. After concluding the call, Vickie contacted a CBMC staff member in the woman's city and arranged for someone to help her get off to a good start in her new spiritual journey.

Who knows how many hurting people were listening to our radio interview? We couldn't help them all, but through Vickie's sensitive and willing spirit, we were able to make a difference for at least one.

Who are the "starfish" God has put into your life? Perhaps it's an employee or a coworker, even one you don't even like very much. Maybe a neighbor next door or across the street, or even someone sitting next to you at church.

If we look at the great spiritual needs in our communities, let alone across America or around the world, it's easy to feel overwhelmed, even defeated. But our job is not the multitudes—that's up to God. Our responsibility is to help a lonely "starfish" or two, responding to their silent cries for help before the sun comes up and the tide goes out.

Phil Downer is President of the Christian Business Men's Committee of USA (CBMC), based in Chattanooga, Tennessee. He is an author of five books, including Eternal Impact: Investing in the Lives of Men, and the newly released, A Father's Reward: Raising Your Children to Walk With God, both published by Harvest House Publishers, Eugene, Oregon. For more information about CBMC or its many resources for evangelism and discipleship in the business world, call 1-800-566-CBMC, or visit the web sites, www.cbmc.com and www.livingproof.com.